English Men of Letters

GEORGE MEREDITH

THE MACMILLAN COMPANY
NEW YORK · BOSTON · CHICAGO · DALLAS
ATLANTA · SAN FRANCISCO

MACMILLAN & CO., Limited
LONDON · BOMBAY · CALCUTTA
MELBOURNE

THE MACMILLAN CO. OF CANADA, Ltd.
TORONTO

GEORGE MEREDITH

BY

J. B. PRIESTLEY

𝔑𝔢𝔴 𝔜𝔬𝔯𝔨

THE MACMILLAN COMPANY

1926

41933

Priestley, John Boynton, 1894–
George Meredith, by J. B. Priestley. New York, Macmillan, 1926. St. Clair Shores, Mich., Scholarly Press, 1970.

vi, 204 p. 21 cm. (English men of letters)

1. Meredith, George, 1828–1909.

PR5013.P7 1970   823′.8   70–131807
ISBN 0–403–00694–5   MARC
Library of Congress   70 ₍4₎

PREFACE

IF the main purpose of this book had been biographical and not critical, I should not have had the audacity to attempt it, as there are still many persons alive who knew Meredith more or less intimately, whereas I have never set eyes upon him and was only a school-boy when he died. But as the chief business of this volume, like the others in the series, is criticism, and criticism, so far as it is possible, aloof from the turmoil of contemporary opinion, I believe my disability as a biographer to be in my favour as a critic. It is difficult for a person who has come into contact with a strong and individual personality such as Meredith even to begin a critical estimate with any degree of impartiality: the man has turned the scale, one way or the other, for the writer. And few writers have suffered more from a lack of detachment in their critics than George Meredith. But whatever my own weaknesses as a critic may be, I have at least here the advantage of impartiality; it requires no effort to be detached; and if it is the opinion of posterity that is required in such a study as this, so far as Meredith is concerned I am free to count my own as one of

v

posterity's voices, though it should be only one of the weakest and most foolish.

The biographical records of Meredith are still rather scanty, but I must acknowledge my debt, for the biographical chapters in this volume, to the Introduction to *The Letters of George Meredith* by his son, Mr. William Maxse Meredith, the biography by Mr. S. M. Ellis, and Mr. J. A. Hammerton's *George Meredith in Anecdote and Criticism.* In the critical chapters, particularly those on his attitude and his poetry, I have been considerably helped by Mr. Trevelyan's *The Poetry and Philosophy of George Meredith* and by Mr. Basil de Sélincourt's study of the poetry included in Mrs. Sturge Henderson's *George Meredith, Novelist, Poet, Reformer.* In addition, I must thank Mr. William Maxse Meredith for correcting certain biographical details and adding others, though it is only fair to him to say that he strongly dissents from many of my opinions. Finally, I must thank Messrs. Constable for permission to make use of the numerous quotations that will be found in the volume.

CONTENTS

CHAPTER I

HIS FAMILY AND EARLY LIFE

I was not until after George Meredith's death that the facts of his parentage, birth and early life were made known to the public. Before that the contemporary books of reference and writers of critical studies told us little more than that he was born "in Hampshire", which suggests either that the reading public was unusually incurious or that the writer himself wished to conceal the facts of his origin and early life. His friend Mr. Edward Clodd has told how he helped Meredith to fill in a census form, and how the latter, after suggesting a vague "Hampshire" as an answer to the birthplace query, finally compromised on "near Petersfield", whereas he was actually born at Portsmouth. Even at the end of his life, when he was England's veteran man of letters and a great European figure, Meredith never seems to have departed from this extraordinary reticence. It was not without its consequences. The same friend has remarked: "Myths rarely accrete round men of note until they die, but Meredith's reticence about his parentage and birthplace gave rise to a host of legends during his lifetime, none of which he was at pains to dispel". The persons who believed some of these fantastic legends were probably influenced by what they had found in Meredith's fiction, and their method of approach to the mystery was by no means foolish. Their mistake was to examine the wrong book, for instead of fastening upon *Harry Richmond,* they should have fastened upon an earlier novel, *Evan Harrington,* in which the truth was not merely revealed but shouted at the top of the writer's voice. There he hardly makes any attempt to cover his tracks, less indeed than the ordinary novelist who is making use of persons and incidents from real life. The "Great Mel" is Melchizedek Meredith, the novelist's grandfather, and his three daughters, Louisa, Harriet, and Caroline, are Meredith's aunts, Louisa, Harriet, and Catherine. The "Lymport" of the novel is, of course, Portsmouth, where the Merediths had their naval outfitter's shop, at No. 73 High Street. At the very outset we are faced with this curious contradiction, for here is a man who appears anxious to conceal the facts of his origin, even at the end of a long and distinguished literary career, and yet practically begins that career by turning the whole matter, both the facts of his origin and his own and his family's feelings on the subject, into a comic novel, a novel that makes light of even the customary reticences of fiction.

What is the explanation? Are we to believe, as some of his acquaintances would have us believe, that to the end of his days this great philosophic poet and novelist, this subtle moralist, was simply ashamed of his connection with a naval outfitter's shop? Mr. S. M. Ellis scouts this theory, and Mr. Ellis deserves to be listened to with respect, because he is a member of the same family (the son of Meredith's cousin, and the great-grandson of the "Great Mel" himself), and further because it was he, in his biography of Meredith, who first discussed the matter. Mr. Ellis suggests that Meredith's use of family history in *Evan Harrington* refutes the theory that he was literally ashamed of the tailor's shop, and asks us to believe that the cause of Meredith's reticence was "an abnormally acute sensitiveness of mind which strove to put aside and forget the memories of old unhappy things". He points out, with some truth, that Meredith's early experiences were extremely unhappy and that, regarding them only with bitterness and pain, he had a natural desire to let them remain obscured. This might explain why he rarely spoke of his early life and his family, but it is not a very satisfactory explanation why he deliberately chose to make a mystery of the matter. A man does not falsify his returns on the census paper, as Meredith did, because he has had an unhappy boyhood. The fact is that it was probably neither plain snobbery, on the one hand, nor extreme sensitiveness, on the other, that prevented Meredith from telling the truth even in his later life. It was a combination of the two, a fear of appearing ridiculous, of producing a comic anti-climax. In later years he was probably ashamed, not of the tailor's shop, but of his shame of the tailor's shop. At one time, let us say during the ten years previous to his writing *Evan Harrington,* when he was a dashing young poet who had come from nowhere but went everywhere, a splendid, handsome young creature at large, when he had quarrelled and lost touch with his family and had no intention of allowing its shears and tape-measure to hang around his neck, it is more than likely that he was ashamed of his origin, deliberately strove to conceal it, and even hinted, in the manner of the Countess de Saldar, at magnificent mysteries in his birth and parentage. *Evan Harrington,* in which the comedy is made plain, is probably the final seal set upon that period. But the comedy he had begun in his life had to be played out. The moment for letting the tailor out of the bag was continually postponed until the very thought of it was impossible. It meant that the mystery of his origin, now lit with romantic legends, would vanish while, amid laughter, there were seen behind him the tailor's shop and the tavern —a notable anti-climax. Further, it meant that he would be compelled to publish his former shame, and by this time he was probably heartily ashamed of that shame. It might be difficult for the handsome young poet to confess the tailor, but it would be still more difficult for the social philosopher and satirist to confess the snob that once lived in him. Years and fame, bringing him under the searchlight, only augmented the danger of confession, for they increased the mystery and therefore heightened the anti-climax. There was nothing for it but to be secretive to the very last. There was in Meredith the writer an intellectual honesty that delighted in pouncing upon and exposing a policy such as this, and it was this quality of his mind that dictated *Evan Harrington,* which is an exposure beyond the wit and malice of his most merciless critics; but there was, too, in Meredith the man a desire to be different from the ordinary not in one but in every particular, a love of mystery and a dark oracular manner, that would make him take kindly, in spite of the derision of his more honest and philosophic self, to this necessary policy of reticence. The latter may or may not be typical of the man, but certainly the lengthy and complete exposure of himself is typical of the writer, as we shall see, and over and above his unusual gifts, it is this self-knowledge that makes him the great creator of Comedy he is. This curious contradiction that we have encountered at the very outset brings us close to the secret of Meredith.

The Merediths were undoubtedly of Welsh origin (and, as usual, preserved a tradition of aristocratic forebears), but they had been settled in Hampshire for several generations before the poet appeared upon the scene, and such Welsh blood as they possessed must by that time have been well mixed with honest Saxon. His grandfather, Melchizedek, was born at Portsea (now merged into Portsmouth) in 1763, and, on attaining his majority, married a woman some ten years older than himself, the daughter of a lawyer in the neighbourhood, and then set up his shop, as a tailor and naval outfitter, at No. 73 High Street, Portsmouth. His business grew to be cne of the best, if not the best, of its kind in the town, and is mentioned by Marryat in *Peter Simple*: "We called at Meredith's, the tailor, and he promised that, by next morning, we should be fitted complete"; and in a letter by Admiral Hardy to his brother: "I can give you a bed. I am at Meradith's (*sic*), the tailor, 73 High Street, opposite the Parade Coffee House." His portrait has been painted for us as the "Great Mel". He was a tall, handsome figure of a man, who had a large social acquaintance, kept horses and hunted, and was an officer in the local Yeomanry.

Whether all the "Great Mel's" expansive gestures, such as that of never sending in a bill, were his, we shall never know, but it is more than likely that George Meredith relied more upon memory than invention, and gave us his grandfather as family and local gossip remembered him. Melchizedek had seven children, two sons and five daughters. Charles, the elder son, died very young. Two of the daughters married local men, but the remaining three went farther afield. Louisa, the most brilliant, married a naval purser named Read, who finally became Consul-General in the Azores and a friend of Pedro, Emperor of Brazil and King of Portugal, who created him a Knight of the Order of the Tower and Sword. Their daughter married Antonio da Costa Cabral, afterwards Marquis de Thomar. This Mrs. Read is, of course, the Louisa, Countess de Saldar, of *Evan Harrington*. Her sister Harriet married John Hellyet, of Surrey, a brewer, and was transformed into the Mrs. Andrew Cogglesby of the novel. The remaining sister, Catherine, became the wife of Samuel Burdon Ellis, a lieutenant in the Royal Marines who afterwards rose to be a General, and who seems to have been libelled rather than portrayed in *Evan Harrington* as Major Strike. His eldest son, George Ellis, was the original of Crossjay Patterne in *The Egoist*. There still remains one of Melchizedek's seven children to be disposed of, namely, the younger son, Augustus Urmston Meredith, born in 1797. He was only seventeen when his dashing father, by this time financially embarrassed, quitted this life at the early age of fifty-one, leaving his widow, a good woman of affairs, and his young son, who had no love of tailoring and was being trained as a doctor, to carry on the business. A few years later Augustus married Jane Eliza Macnamara, the daughter of Michael Macnamara, a local innkeeper, and said to have been a very handsome and refined woman. She was not, as Meredith afterwards said she was, "pure Irish", as her mother was certainly English; and it is more than likely that, in spite of all Meredith's talk of the Celtic strain in him, the Irish blood in his mother had been as well mixed with English as had the Welsh blood in his father. To Augustus Meredith and his wife there was born, on the 12th February 1828, a son, their only child, George Meredith.

Some slight records of Meredith's childhood and boyhood remain to us. We know that he was con- sidered proud and stand-offish by the other boys in the neighbourhood, the sons of High Street tradesmen, and that at one time he was known to them as "Gentle- man Georgy". Meredith was to rise to undreamed-of heights, to become at length the most distinguished living writer in England, but it is doubtful if he did not always remain "Gentleman Georgy". Certain weaknesses that always stayed with Meredith, the man if not the writer, are suggested by that signifi- cant nickname. It is the "Gentleman Georgy" in Mere- dith that has prejudiced so many readers. But the circumstances of his childhood were not altogether favourable to him, and possibly account for some of his less admirable traits of character. He was an only child, and a very handsome, precocious child. His mother died when he was only five, and he and his father were never in sympathy. The

Merediths were in a curious position, somewhere
between fish and fowl, for they considered themselves
the social superiors of the other tradespeople of the
High Street, and yet were not quite "gentry", so that
they floated, uneasily, in a social mid-air. Never
knowing exactly where they stood, they would naturally
be far more sensitive and touchy than persons with a
more closely defined status in local society. An only
child of such people would be brought up in a not
altogether healthy, somewhat tropical atmosphere, for
he would be compelled to spend most of his time either
alone or in the company of his elders, who would
encourage him to regard himself as some one different
from the ordinary, a creature apart. A great deal of
the later Meredith can be explained, without making
use of a fantastic theory of psychology, in terms of this
early upbringing of his. There are, however, com-
pensations, for a child so situated is under the necessity
of developing his own resources and so contrives to
live richly in his imagination, which is precisely what
Meredith did, according to his own account of his
childhood. Nearly all extremely creative men of
genius, men who, later in life, have had the capacity
of living intensely with the creatures of their imagination, seem to have been deprived of a normally happy
and healthy childhood, which would not have driven
them, as they were driven, to compensate themselves
for the lack of companionship and outward incident
by an early life of dreams and fantasies.

In 1833, at the early age of thirty-one, Mrs.
Meredith died, so that George was now left to the
companionship of his father and an adult cousin.
Augustus Meredith appears to have been a pleasant,

cultured man, fond of walking, reading, chess, and
society, though without the force of character of his
father, the "Great Mel", or his son, who probably
inherited more from his paternal grandfather than from
his father. George, at the age of nine, was sent to a
local high school, St. Paul's School, Southsea, but
a few years later his father married his house-
keeper, and, discovering that he could not succeed
with the Portsmouth shop, sold the business and
moved to London. By 1846 he was established in a
tailoring business at 26 St. James's Street. Meanwhile, George had been left behind and sent to
school, but in 1842 the trustee of his mother's
small estate, of which he was the heir, determined to
send him to the Moravian School at Neuwied, and it
was in the August of that year that the fourteen-year-
old boy entered the school and began his real education.
This school deserves a word to itself. Neuwied, a
little town in the most romantic part of the Rhine
country, was one of those little German principalities
that became centres of social progress and culture.
Its Moravian school was founded during the reign
of a liberal-minded eighteenth-century prince who
believed in religious tolerance and allowed every
religious sect the fullest liberty of thought and worship,
and so excellent was the course of education offered by
the Moravian Brethren in Neuwied, so inspiring their
influence, that their school soon became famous and
attracted pupils from all parts of Western Europe. In
addition to Meredith, several Englishmen of note were
educated there, and, indeed, the decade previous to
Meredith's stay there was known as "the English
Period". Professor Henry Morley, himself an old

scholar who left the school a few years before Meredith arrived there, declared half a century later, at a gathering of "Old Neuwieders", that "no formal process of education had acted upon their lives so thoroughly or so much for their good as the little time they had spent at Neuwied. It had taken all the bitterness out of their lives, all envy and hatred and uncharitableness having been so thoroughly removed from them by contact with the gentle spirit of the old Moravians." It was here that Meredith spent two years, without a break, during the most formative period of a man's life, and it would be difficult to overestimate the importance of these two years.

The Germany he saw was the Germany of the year immediately preceding '48, when an enthusiastic and romantic liberalism and nationalism were fermenting the educated classes, when social service was becoming the ideal of romantic young men, when liberalism had penetrated into theology, and free thought was in the air. The very fact of going abroad at all to be educated meant that Meredith had an opportunity to escape that provincialism which Arnold was later to denounce as one of the most glaring faults of the age; and the fact that he went to Germany, and to a centre of liberalism, nationalism, and religious tolerance, partly explains the bent of his mind and the curious way in which he seems to escape his age. Meredith owed Germany a great deal more than the inspiration for *Farina* or the German scenes in *Harry Richmond*; it shaped his mind and determined the course of his thought and gave him a certain romanticism that coloured all his work, no matter how purely intellectual, how much in the spirit of pure comedy,

the underlying conception of that work might be.   It
is difficult to decide where this influence ends.   Even
that wilfulness, love of the fantastic, particularly in
matters of construction and style, indifference to form,
all of which mark his work both in poetry and fiction,
may have their root in German influences.   Thus, the
influence of Jean Paul Richter is plainly apparent
in him, as it is in Carlyle.   Along with these positive
results may be ranged certain negative ones.   He
escaped the common public-school-university course
of education, and he displays, perhaps in a heightened
form, the virtues and defects of most clever men who
have escaped from the normal educational course, for
he is markedly original and brilliant, but is ever in
danger of becoming merely wilful, deliberately formless,
and unnecessarily fantastic, a man who will never
quite come to terms either with his fellows or with the
material of his art.   Meredith is one of those dazzling
artists who are much criticised, but always as if they
are visitants from another planet and not men with a
significant biography behind them; and unfortunately
this is not the place in which to begin a study of his
mind and art in terms of his personal history, particularly his early life and the influences that played upon
it.   But when that study comes to be written, it will
be found that those two years at Neuwied must
inevitably be given a very prominent place.

On leaving Neuwied in 1844, Meredith must have
joined his father in London, but we know nothing of
his movements until two years later, when we find him
articled to one Richard Stephen Charnock, a solicitor
in Paternoster Row.   It was a foregone conclusion
that the handsome, brilliant boy, who had begun to

scribble verses and had still a little money left from his mother's legacy, would not remain long in a solicitor's office; but his association with Charnock, a member of the Arundel Club and a man of some reading, seems to have done him more good than harm, for it was Charnock who introduced him to a little set of literary aspirants who revolved about a manuscript magazine (handed round to the contributors and criticised by them) entitled the *Monthly Observer*. It was in this magazine, in the April number for 1849, that Meredith's first published poem, "Chillian-wallah", appears. Three months later, this poem, of topical interest but of no merit, was accepted and printed by *Chambers's Journal*. Meanwhile Meredith had gone into lodgings in Ebury Street for his father had now left London for Cape Town, where he once more set up his tailor's shop, and where, eleven years later, he read *Evan Harrington* and was "pained, beyond expression". In 1863 Augustus Meredith returned to England, retiring to Portsmouth, where he lived until his death in 1876. It is said that Meredith occasionally paid a short visit to his father when the latter returned to this country, but such visits were mere duty-calls, for the two had been long estranged, and all affection, at least on the son's part, had waned long ago. It was not long after his father's departure for South Africa and his own coming of age that Meredith made what can only be called his amazing marriage. Among his friends of the *Monthly Observer* set was Edward Gryffydh Peacock, son of the famous Thomas Love Peacock, novelist, poet, and East India Examiner. The two young men went long walks together and visited one another's rooms. They were

soon joined in their walks and discussions by a third
person, Edward Peacock's sister, Mary Ellen Nicholls,
the widow of a naval officer, a witty and beautiful
woman of thirty. She and Meredith had much in
common, and soon the young poet was passionately in
love, and, overlooking the lady's nine years' seniority
(and she had a daughter of five) and his own lack of
means or prospects, was proposing marriage. Six
times, it is said, she refused him, but the brilliant
youngster's persistence and impetuosity swept away
her doubts and scruples, and finally they were married
at St. George's, Hanover Square, in August 1849. For
some time they lived abroad and then with Thomas
Love Peacock or in lodgings at the seaside. During one
period they made their home with a Mrs. Macirone
(whose daughter, Emilia, supplied Meredith with some
suggestions for a future heroine, Emilia Sandra
Belloni) at The Limes, Weybridge, where the Merediths met a number of literary people, Bulwer Lytton,
R. H. Horne, Tom Taylor, and others. And living
nearby was a family that provided Meredith with one
of his most lasting friendships, Sir Alexander and Lady
Duff Gordon and their little daughter Janet, afterwards
Mrs. Ross, with whom Meredith was ever afterwards
on most affectionate terms.

Both husband and wife were writing hard, sometimes
in collaboration. They produced, between them, a
little work on the Art of Cookery, a subject in which
they were both interested and one that undoubtedly
would receive a great deal of attention in any house
occupied by Thomas Love Peacock. But most of
their time was devoted to verse. Meredith had
received an introduction to Dickens and contributed

a certain number of poems to *Household Words.* Two
poems were also published by *Fraser's Magazine.* It
was the publisher of *Fraser's,* J. W. Parker, who
brought out, in the summer of 1851, the *Poems*—Meredith's first book. It was produced at the author's own
expense and cost him a sixty pounds that he could ill
afford. Afterwards Meredith came to dislike this
little volume (which was dedicated to his father-in-
law) and would not hear it mentioned, but though it
contained a good deal of very poor *juvenilia,* it also
contained, among other good things, the first version of
"Love in the Valley". Tennyson read the book and
wrote to Meredith expressing his delight in the haunting cadences of "Love in the Valley". But the little
book that first gave the world this lovely song of youthful passion was a distinct failure. Such reviews as it
obtained were merely perfunctory, with the exception
of a notice in the *Critic* by William Michael Rossetti,
then a youngster of twenty-one, and a review by
Kingsley in *Fraser's.* The latter praised the love
lyrics and observed that "health and sweetness are
two qualities which run through all these poems". A
letter from the greatest poet of the day and at least one
long considered notice, for the most part eulogistic, by
a well-known man of letters is by no means a bad
beginning for a poet of twenty-three, but Meredith,
though he had made light of the book's prospects in
discussing it with his publisher and friends, was at
heart bitterly disappointed at its reception, all the more
so because he could ill afford to lose the money he had
spent on its production.

Two years after the publication of the *Poems* the
Merediths removed from Weybridge to Lower Halli-

ford, to live with Peacock, now a widower. Here their
son, Arthur Gryffydh, was born in June 1853. There
had been several children before this, but they had died
in infancy. But a baby, an exhuberant and restless son-
in-law, a young couple given to hot disputes and
quarrels, were too much for Peacock, a comfortable
old Epicurean of sixty-eight, and so the Merediths
moved across the way into Vine Cottage, leaving the
old humorist in peace with his wine and his Greek.
Something must be said of this association of Meredith's with Peacock, an association of some importance,
because Peacock, with the weight of his forty-three
years' seniority, his prestige both as a writer and the
companion of Shelley and others, his very clearly
defined attitude towards life and literature, must have
had a considerable influence upon his young and
impressionable son-in-law. Unfortunately we know
little of this association, because Meredith, after the
disaster of his first marriage, to which we are coming,
refused to talk about it, and as Peacock was intimately
connected with this marriage, naturally Meredith rarely
discussed his friendship with the older writer. There
are, of course, traces of Peacock himself in some of
Meredith's characters, notably Dr. Middleton. It is
not, however, as a character to be portrayed but as a
literary influence that Peacock is important in Meredith's life. What was it that turned the attention of
this romantic young poet to intellectual comedy? The
Essay on Comedy shows that Meredith had made a
close study of the subject, and his fiction, from the very
beginning shows a determination to fuse romantic narrative with high comedy. The native bent of his
mind will partly explain the direction taken by his

genius, but something must be allowed for the influence of Peacock himself, a notable and indefatigable servant of the Comic Spirit and a close and enthusiastic student of comedy in all its forms, particularly Greek comedy, with which Meredith's fiction, in spite of radical differences of form, has some curious affinities. We know that Meredith admired Peacock's comic novels, and it would be impossible for so young and impressionable a man to be in close contact with a forceful personality like Peacock and not be influenced by his point of view and opinions. Meredith's long service to the Comic Spirit, to which he dedicated a richer mind and a greater genius than ever Peacock possessed, probably began over the madeira and port in Peacock's study. The marriage with the daughter may have been a disaster to Meredith the man, but the association with the father was undoubtedly a godsend to Meredith the writer.

This marriage was doomed from the outset. It was not so much the difference in age as the likeness in temperament that made it disastrous. Both husband and wife were of the same kind, brilliant, ambitious, highly strung, uncompromising, bitter-tongued, so that there was no point of rest between them, no possibility of give and take, no mutual adjustment of wills and purpose. The conditions of their married life were not likely to make things easier, being a dreary sequence of duns, lodgings, dead babies, and baffled literary ambition. There were frequent quarrels and scenes, separations and reconciliations, until at last, in 1858, Mrs. Meredith left the country with an artist named Wallis. Her boy, Arthur, remained with his father. In 1859 she returned to this country, a sick, brooding, and sorrowful woman, aching for the child that had been taken away from her, living in lodgings at Twickenham, Hastings, Seaford, and Weybridge, where she died, friendless, in October 1861. Meredith did not visit her during her last illness and did not attend the funeral. He was always reticent on the subject of this tragic marriage, merely remarking, "No sun warmed my roof-tree; the marriage was a blunder; she was nine years my senior"; and suggesting that there was a taint of madness in the Peacock family. Once more it is to his work that we must turn if we wish to learn more; Meredith the poet opened his heart when Meredith the man closed his lips; and there, in "Modern Love", written not long after the death of Mrs. Meredith, is not a little of his private history. The tragedy compelled him to search his memory and mind and heart, and the result of this self-examination (with certain allowances for drama) may be found in that subtly introspective, almost self-torturing poem. Once again we are faced with that curious contradiction which runs through the life of Meredith. The man himself does not come out of this disastrous affair too well, for he showed himself somewhat cold and implacable in the face of suffering and sorrow that reduced his own injuries to mere trifles: his pride would not allow him to speak the forgiving word and make the generous gesture. But the poet in him could not be made a party to this conspiracy of cold silence, and he traces, with a rare subtlety and sympathy, the course of a tragedy that shows us, not an erring wife and a wronged husband, but simply two unhappy lovers inevitably drifting apart. It has been said that, after this catastrophe, Meredith became for a time. something of a misogynist, levelling the sharp arrows of his wit against the creature Woman. But whatever the man may have said and done, the writer certainly took up a very different attitude. Meredith, in his work may have missed many opportunities, but he never afterwards missed an opportunity of championing a woman, and the arrows of his wit, still quivering in the mark, are those that can be seen transfixing complacent, tyrannical, and egoistical males.

During the period covered by the preceding paragraphs, the 'fifties, Meredith had been busy writing, both in prose and verse. In the middle of the decade *The Shaving of Shagpat* was published by Chapman & Hall. Among the reviews was one by George Eliot in the *Leader*, an enthusiastic notice that welcomed the tale as "a work of genius and of poetical genius". The reviews on the whole were favourable, but the public took but a languid interest in this curious mixture of pure Oriental fantasy and allegory and it was a long time before the first edition was exhausted. At this time Meredith was living with Maurice Fitz-Gerald, nephew of Edward FitzGerald, and a scholar and gourmet (the original of the Wise Youth in *Richard Feverel*), at the decayed little seaside town of Seaford. *The House on the Beach* was begun here, but it was not finished and published until the later 'seventies. Meredith and his gastronomical young friend had discovered a wonderful cook in the person of the village carpenter's wife, and with her they lodged, to plan dinners and talk literature. Here, in 1857, he wrote *Farina: A Legend of Cologne,* which was brought out by Smith, Elder & Co. in the autumn of that year. *Farina,* the slightest and least admired of all Meredith's tales, was even less successful than *The Shaving of Shagpat.* There are good reasons for this, as the blend of a Gothic tale of terror, farce, and vague allegory of which the story is composed is not a happy one, though there are some good things in the book, notably the fine passages of description in which Meredith makes good use of his memories of the Rhine country. George Eliot noticed the book in the *Westminster Review,* and, though clearly favourably disposed towards its author, with whom she was now acquainted, was compelled to admit a falling-off from the standard of *Shagpat.*

The following year, after his wife's flight to Capri, Meredith moved to London with his young son, Arthur, taking rooms in Hobury Street, Chelsea. For a year he occupied himself with his first long novel, *Richard Feverel,* which was finally completed and published, by Chapman & Hall, in 1859. Its appearance marks the arrival of Meredith the novelist and social philosopher. *The Times* gave it a review three columns long. This fact should be stressed because that legend of early neglect, fostered by Meredith himself, still survives. Actually the conditions under which Meredith began his literary career were far more favourable to a man of his genius and temperament than the conditions prevailing to-day. A contemporary novelist of thirty-one years of age—or, indeed, of any age—would not know what to do with himself if he found that a novel of his had been given a three-column review in *The Times.* Moreover—to settle the question once for all—Meredith's succeeding stories were serialised in the most important periodicals of the time, and though these stories had not, of course, the success they deserved in book form for many years, yet he was by no means ungenerously treated by his publishers. We do not know what income Meredith derived from his fiction during the first ten years or so of his career as a novelist, but in view of the serial publication of these long stories, such as *Evan Harrington* and *Vittoria,* in prosperous periodicals, he would be a bold man who would declare that Meredith would have been more fortunate if he had been born fifty or sixty years later. Among other distinguished readers of *Richard Feverel* soon after its publication were Carlyle and his wife. Carlyle was sufficiently interested to write to the publishers for information about the author, with the result that Meredith, who was living close at hand, called at Cheyne Row and made Carlyle's acquaintance. There are actually distinct traces of Carlyle's influence in the style of *Richard Feverel,* a style that Meredith later condemned as "lumpy". About this time, too, Meredith began another acquaintance that very quickly ripened into a lasting friendship. This was with Captain (afterwards Rear-Admiral) Frederick Augustus Maxse, a young naval officer who had distinguished himself in the Crimean War and was deeply interested in literature and social philosophy. He is, of course, the original of that Beauchamp whose career as a naval officer turned Radical candidate was to be the subject of one of Meredith's greatest novels. The two young men went for a cruise in Maxse's little yacht, and enjoyed together their common passion for lengthy walks and talks. It was this new friendship that took Meredith, in 1859, to Surrey, first at Esher, and then to Copsham Cottage, between Esher and Oxshott.

Although there is no truth in the legend that Meredith wrote his early novels living in a garret on oatmeal and water, and a good deal of evidence to show that during this period he was living comfortably and indulging his taste in good food and good wine, it must be admitted that he was only able to maintain himself even in a moderate standard of comfort by doing hack work of various kinds. His early fiction was by no means so unproductive as is frequently supposed, but he needed other sources of income. These he began to tap during this period. The first and the slightest of these extra-literary occupations was, fantastically enough, reading to an old lady. This was Mrs. Benjamin Wood, of Eltham Lodge, an elderly lady who was a scholar and something of an authoress, whom Meredith visited for some time, usually twice a week, in the capacity of reader. It says something for Meredith that he contrived to give satisfaction in this very un-Olympian task, and that he and his employer became very good friends. The next step was more important. In 1860 Meredith became a regular contributor to the *Ipswich Journal*, an old-established Conservative newspaper, whose proprietor, a barrister named Foakes, was an acquaintance of his. He remained on the staff of this paper for eight years, at a salary of about £200 a year. His task was to contribute leading articles and a summary of the week's news, that is, the news outside Suffolk, and he made a practice of going up to London every Thursday to see either the proprietor or the paper's London representative and to finish off and hand in his "copy". Some of these contributions, unsigned, of course, but showing unmistakable traces of Meredith's manner, have been dragged into the light by those well-meaning enthusiasts who contrive, before they have done, to make the object of their veneration wish they had never been born. These extracts, gibes at Lincoln and the "Yankees" (the American Civil War being the most important topic of the time), and John Bright, and so forth, make very strange reading in the face of Meredith's pronounced Radical views. The odd thing is not so much the fact that Meredith could write on the opposite side, but that he could put forward views so contrary to his own real opinions with such extraordinary gusto. There may have been a smack of irony in it, but it is more likely that Meredith was able to do it simply because such political convictions as he had during this period were a trifle shadowy when compared with the solid advantages of £200 a year. Possibly his Radical convictions were held far more strongly after 1868, but even then his almost enthusiastic weekly apostasy during the eight years he was connected with the *Ipswich Journal* is a little difficult to explain. During this same period he occasionally contributed articles to another and more important Conservative organ, the *Morning Post*, and it was as the special correspondent of this paper that Meredith went to the Italian front during the campaign of 1866. His articles may be found in the volume of miscellaneous prose in the Collected Edition, but they are of no great interest, being merely the painstaking but somewhat dull and stilted accounts of a man who was anything but a war correspondent. After his return from Italy, in the later months of 1867, he took the editorial chair of the *Fortnightly Review*, to which he contributed poems and reviews, for his friend John Morley, who was absent in America. A little later he did some work for the *Pall Mall Gazette*. This is the extent of his journalism, and as soon as he was able to dispense with it he did so, as he had no aptitude for newspaper work and, in spite of his great gifts, was not sufficiently adaptable to make even a moderate success of it. His heart was elsewhere, and ever afterwards journalism spelt drudgery to him, and he never mentioned it but with a wry mouth.

The very year that saw him turn journalist also saw him established as literary adviser, in the place of John Forster, to his publishers, Chapman & Hall. Reading manuscripts he found an easier and more congenial task than writing leaders, and he remained with Chapman & Hall for thirty-five years, long after he had attained celebrity as a novelist. In those days, when publishing was a more leisurely and personal affair than it is now, a publisher's reader had far more influence and authority than he has at the present time. He adopted a paternal attitude, frequently suggested emendations, and not seldom discussed their work with the authors themselves. Several writers, among them no less a person than Thomas Hardy, met Meredith in his capacity as reader, and have left on record their impressions of him. In addition, we know from Chapman & Hall's record of his reports, which have been preserved, something of his history as a critic of unpublished work. On the whole, though he was very painstaking and occasionally showed great critical acuteness, it speaks well for the loyalty of the publishers, a loyalty probably based on admiration of the writer, that he was with them so long, for a less gifted person would have better served their turn. A short list of some of the better-known books and authors he rejected or recommended is surprising. That he should have summarily rejected such writers as Mrs. Henry Wood and Ouida was a misfortune for his publishers (he rejected *East Lynne* twice, and it was, of course, a gold mine for its publishers), but does not surprise us. But it is odd that he should have been able to see the merit or promise in the early work of Hardy, Gissing, Olive Schreiner (with whom he talked over *The Story of an African Farm* and suggested certain alterations), and yet curtly condemned such things as Butler's *Erewhon* and the early novels of Bernard Shaw, things faulty enough but bristling with promise.

The fact is that though Meredith, on a subject that he had made his own, such as Comedy, could at times display all the qualities of a great critic, he was too preoccupied with his own creative work, too seldom given to laying his own mind open to other minds, and rather in too great a hurry to deliver judgement to be even a satisfactory critic. Some of his remarks about fellow-authors, such as his opinion that "not much of Dickens will live, because it has so little correspondence to life", and so forth, are easily the most foolish he ever made or at least of which we have any record. It was in his capacity as publishers' reader that Meredith made his one and only appearance in a court of law, being called as an expert witness, in 1891, when one of Chapman & Hall's authors, whose work he had recommended, was considered to have libelled a certain James Pinnock, who brought an action against the publishers. Meredith was cross-examined by the formidable Sir Charles Russell and acquitted himself very well, at the same time giving *Punch* an excellent opportunity for a literary cartoon and parody. It is somewhat ironical that Meredith should have been giving evidence for an unfortunate author who actually had only been tripped up by a coincidence, for the distinguished novelist in the witness-box had been putting all his relatives, friends and acquaintances to good uses in his fiction for half a lifetime. Oddly enough, too, we have it from Mr. S. B. Ellis that the defendant in this case, Colonel Ellis, was actually a son of the Major Strike of *Evan Harrington* (the Major-General Ellis already mentioned, who married again after the death of his first wife, Meredith's aunt), so that the two men, though unaware of the fact, were actually related by marriage. Thus Colonel Ellis's most important witness was the man who had undoubtedly libelled his father as Major Strike in a novel thirty-odd years before. One step further and we should be plunged into something not unlike Meredithian comedy itself.

This account of Meredith's activities as journalist and publishers' reader has taken us a long way from the time when he first began them, in 1860 at Esher, and thither we must return. Here at Esher he encountered again his old friends, Lady Duff Gordon and her daughter Janet, now a girl of sixteen, both of whom he put into his next novel, *Evan Harrington*, as Lady Jocelyn and Rose. At this time he was contributing poems, mostly of the lighter sort, such as "Juggling Jerry", to *Once a Week*, in which they were illustrated by Tenniel, Millais, and Sandys. This brought Meredith into touch with the Pre-Raphaelite group, notably Dante Gabriel Rossetti and Swinburne, then just down from Oxford. Meredith had now removed into Copsham Cottage, a delightful little house by the roadside, surrounded by open country, heath and common, covered with gorse and heather, and fringed with pine woods. Close at hand was a large grassy knoll known as "Round Hill" or "The Mound", a viewpoint that Meredith often frequented and that plays a considerable part in the story of Emilia. So, too, the gipsies and vagabonds who haunted the neighbouring common, found their way into the work that Meredith began at this time, such as "Juggling Jerry" and the other *Poems of the English Roadside*. Some of his very finest poetry, his "Ode to the Spirit of Earth in Autumn" and the rest, was inspired by this glorious countryside, which he came to know by heart in all its moods. Busy as he was, with his poetry and stories, his journalism and publishers' reading, he had time to entertain and be entertained, and this period marks the beginning of several friendships. Through the Duff Gordons he met such celebrities as Mrs. Norton (later to be transformed into Diana Warwick), Kinglake, and G. F. Watts. F. C. Burnand, John Morley, Bonaparte Wyse (grand-nephew of Napoleon and a Provençal poet of some distinction, with whom Meredith later toured the Continent), Lionel Robinson, James Cotter Morison, Augustus Jessopp (to whose school at Norwich Arthur Meredith was sent a little later), and William Hardman were some of the friends Meredith made during this period. The last-named was one of the most important. William Hardman was a Lancashire man who migrated from the Bar into journalism, becoming, in 1872, editor of the *Morning Post*. He and Meredith had in common a love of literature, long walks, and good cooking, and a fund of high spirits, but temperamentally they were very different, as Hardman had a sturdy matter-of-fact mind and was in the habit, as he tells us, of coming down "in the midst of his (Meredith's) poetical rhapsodies with frequent morsels of hard common sense". Luckily for us Hardman was one of those sensible persons who leave on record trustworthy accounts of their intercourse with the great, and he gives us a very vivid picture of Meredith as he was then, in his early thirties.

When this account of Hardman's is supplemented by other records of that time, notably Burnand's description of his first meeting with the poet, we have to hand a portrait of Meredith, as he was in the very prime of his manhood, of considerable value. Like most writers who have lived to a great age, even though it be a magnificently youthful old age, Meredith has suffered somewhat, just as did Wordsworth and Carlyle, and perhaps Tennyson, from the profusion of records of him as an old man, tending as they do to make people forget that he was ever a young one. It is as well to correct the familiar impression of that autumnal, though splendid, figure of Box Hill, by some account of him in the first flush of his ripened manhood, as he appeared to those young men of the early 'sixties who tramped out to Copsham Cottage. All records, from whatever source, agree in presenting a highly attractive figure. A lithe, athletic body, loosely turned out in a flannel shirt, knickerbockers, stout boots, the whole completed by a wide-awake, and a scarlet flowing tie;

a memorably handsome and sensitive face (Rossetti used it as the model for his head of Christ in his Mary Magdalene picture), amply framed in curly red-gold hair, beard, and moustache; a vehement, compelling personality, still with any amount of the boy, ready to walk, talk, and laugh all day and all night, remaining to leaven the wit and philosopher; a man of great mental and physical activity, attacking work and play with immense gusto, tossing up and catching an iron bar (his favourite exercise) or striding over the heaths and hills all day, with a fund of irrepressible high spirit and becoming noisily nonsensical at certain times and in certain companies, with a sharp eye for natural beauty and floods of seasoned talk; the ideal companion for a strenuous walking-tour. This is the figure that emerges from all these records of Meredith as he was in the early 'sixties. It is not, of course, the whole man, for such accounts are of holidays and holiday high spirits, and there is another side of the man to be discovered in "Modern Love" and the other poems of the period. But the high spirits, the healthy activities, the literary companionship of those years combine to present a singularly attractive picture, not easily matched in the records of nineteenth-century men of letters. The Surrey hills seem to resound with laughter and snatches of song and great lines of poetry coming down the south-west wind. Here it was that Swinburne, still half angel, half elf, appeared one day, frantic with excitement, waving a copy of FitzGerald's *Omar*, new from Quaritch's "Twopenny Box", and for hours the two poets and some others sat on "The Mount", as on a peak in Darien, declaiming the exquisite and now so familiar lines. This was the night

that Swinburne, on fire with the day's happenings, began his "Laus Veneris", completing the first thirteen
stanzas in an hour. Poetry was in the very air of the
Surrey uplands during Meredith's Copsham days.

In the early part of 1860 *Once a Week* printed *Evan
Harrington* as a serial, illustrated by Charles Keene,
and during the following year it was brought out in
book form, in three volumes, by Bradbury & Evans.
The story, longer than the version we know now and
somewhat more farcical, for Meredith pruned it later,
does not seem to have called out any noteworthy
criticism, favourable or unfavourable, and would seem
to have attracted less attention than *Richard Feverel.*
But there is more of the essential Meredith in *Richard
Feverel* than in *Evan Harrington*, which, perhaps owing
to the fact that it may have been planned earlier,
always seems the younger and more uncertain book of
the two. Shortly after the publication of his second
novel, Meredith travelled in Germany, Switzerland, and
Italy, accompanied by his little boy, Arthur, to whom
he was at this time intensely devoted. The boy was
not very strong, and needed constant care, and Meredith
himself had not been too well, but they both returned
in excellent health, and Meredith was able to complete
his new volume of poems, *Modern Love and Poems of
the English Roadside*, in time for the spring of 1862.
The book, which contains some of his finest poetry,
excited little comment. The *Spectator,* however, came
out with an adverse criticism, in which the poet is
described as "a clever man, without literary genius,
taste, or judgment", and there is some talk of prurience
and vulgarity. This very foolish notice kindled Swinburne, who immediately wrote one of those letters

protesting against the unfair treatment of other men's
work that were by no means the least of his literary
activities. "Mr. Meredith", wrote Swinburne, "is one
of the three or four poets now alive whose work, perfect or imperfect, is always as noble in design as it
is often faultless in result." Just as Tennyson had
expressed his admiration of the previous volume, so
Browning, who could recognise in several of these
poems a manner not unlike his own, warmly expressed
his admiration of this new volume.

The same month, June, that saw Swinburne's letter
of protest saw the two poets lodged under one roof
with a third. Meredith had to be in London at least
one day a week, and so he took rooms at 16 Cheyne
Walk with Rossetti and Swinburne, completing an odd
and perhaps unique trinity of geniuses and fellow-
boarders. It was not to be expected that this arrange-
ment would endure, even though Meredith only spent
a part of his time in Chelsea. There are a number of
legends centred about this queer *ménage,* one of which
tells us that Meredith left because his companions
treated him to a new pair of boots, and another that he
quitted the house in disgust because Rossetti ate half-
a-dozen eggs for breakfast; but the fact is that Meredith and his two companions found it impossible to live
together without constant friction. They had a genuine
admiration for one another's work, but little in common
beyond that, and all of them were quick to take offence.
Between Meredith and Swinburne, there was a long
coolness, said to be due to the latter's want of appreciation of Meredith's later and more characteristic novels,
and this partial breach was only closed towards the end
of their lives.

After making several summer journeys, Meredith took his son to Norwich to the school of his friend, Dr. Jessopp, afterwards visiting Cambridge. Christmas was spent with the boy in London, when the novelist was very much the devoted and delighted parent, visiting the pantomime on Boxing Day, the Tower, and the Bank of England, and so forth. Measles, an accident to Arthur, and a visit to Seaford in company with several friends make up the history of father and son during the first half of 1863, but in August, Meredith, alone once more, went over to Paris and Grenoble. He returned to Copsham Cottage in the early autumn to grapple with *Emilia in England,* a story that gave him more trouble than any other, and to make the acquaintance of a neighbour, of Huguenot extraction, a Mr. Justin Theodore Vulliamy, and his three daughters. With the youngest of them, Marie, a girl of twenty-four and an excellent musician, a warm friendship began, which was only deepened by an encounter in Norwich, where they both happened to be staying and where they did some "cathedralising" together, followed by a journey back to London in one another's company. Shortly afterwards, in the spring of 1864, their engagement was announced, and Meredith's second marriage, destined to be as happy as the first was wretched, took place in the following September in Mickleham church. Few writers have deserved more of Woman than Meredith, for few writers have been so unsparing in their championship of her or so sensitive in their understanding of her qualities and motives, and it was perhaps only just that his first marriage, so ill-advised and unhappy, should have been followed at last by a second that brought perhaps more peace and happiness than

most unions.   Meanwhile, he had published, through
Chapman & Hall, the three volumes of *Emilia in England,* later to be called *Sandra Belloni,* a story on which
he had been engaged, though not continuously, for over
three years, and parts of which he had rewritten more
than once.   The reviews were fuller and more appreciative on the whole than those of the previous novels,
and in two articles, one by Richard Garnett on the
book itself and the other by Justin McCarthy on *Novels
with a Purpose,* there are references that suggest that
Meredith was beginning to be taken for granted as a
brilliant and original novelist, an important moment in
the history of a writer.   In the autumn following its
publication a translation of the story was printed by
the *Revue des Deux Mondes.*

After their marriage Meredith and his wife had
stayed near Southampton, and had then removed to
Norbiton, where they occupied a house opposite that of
their friends the Hardmans.   In this house, Kingston
Lodge, their son, William Maxse, was born in July
1865.   Meredith had allowed his novels to overlap a
good deal during this period, and he was now engaged
in finishing *Rhoda Fleming,* which had been begun four
years earlier, and was wrestling with the sequel to
Emilia—Vittoria.   As Chapman & Hall did not want
another book from him for some months, Meredith sold
Rhoda Fleming to William Tinsley for £400.   The book
does not appear to have sold well and did not attract
much attention.   *Rhoda Fleming* was something of an
experiment, an excursion into unfamiliar country, and
has perhaps been more variously estimated than any
other of Meredith's novels.   There have not been wanting critics who have placed it at the head, or almost

at the head, of his works; but it is significant that
such critics have usually shown themselves indifferent
if not hostile to his more characteristic work. Meredith
himself never rated it very highly, and came to dislike it
so much later in life that he advised a correspondent
not to read it. Once this story was off his hands
he was free to return to *Vittoria,* begun as a sequel
to *Emilia* but carried forward rather as a romance
of Italy in revolt, and largely rewritten with an eye
to an epic movement in place of the usual involved
comedy of character. G. H. Lewes, then editing the
Fortnightly Review, admired the story and accepted
it as a serial, paying Meredith £250 for the rights.
Fortunately Meredith, who wanted some "local colour"
for the story before its final revision for publication
in volume form, was able to travel to Italy as war
correspondent for the *Morning Post* during the summer of 1866. Early in the following year the story
appeared, in three volumes published by Chapman &
Hall, but for some curious reason, curious inasmuch
as the story is one of the most vivid and romantic of
its time, and events in Italy had aroused considerable
excitement here, neither the press nor the public liked
the book, and both publishers and author were compelled to consider it a commercial failure. Here for
once Meredith's bitterness at the lack of appreciation
was justified. The double failure of *Rhoda Fleming*
and *Vittoria* weighed heavily upon him, so much so
that he talked of being compelled to abandon fiction in
favour of journalism. One enthusiastic admirer the
Italian story had, and that, it is hardly necessary to
say, was Swinburne, whose *Song of Italy* had just
appeared and who wrote to Meredith expressing his

enthusiasm. The two men spent a few days together at Kingston Lodge.

But building operations and an unpleasant church organ combined to drive the Merediths away from Kingston Lodge. They discovered, in the country-side they both loved, a house of the kind that most of us only discover in our dreams. It was an old house, standing on a slope of Box Hill, backed by woods and facing a great expanse of open country. A finer situation for a writer to whom the sights and sounds of our Southern England were a passion, whatever the season or the day's mood, could not be imagined. There they removed at the beginning of 1868 to Flint Cottage, Box Hill, the house for ever associated with Meredith's name, where he was to live for more than forty years, where his greatest work was written, and where he died.

CHAPTER II

THE removal to Box Hill marks a natural division
between Meredith's early and later life. From this
time onwards his life is more ordered and settled and
less eventful than it was before, and a record of it is
largely a record of his publications, his growing reputation, and his friendships. His forty-first year found
him happily married, with young children about him,
with a fairly secure position, ready to enter upon the
most fruitful ten or twelve years of his existence.
There was, however, one tragic circumstance in this
new life of his that must be mentioned, although this
is not the place for anything like a full treatment of
it. In the years previous to his second marriage
Meredith had concentrated, with an almost Feverel-like
intensity and unwisdom, upon his young son, Arthur,
a delicate sensitive boy who had reached the age of
eleven when his father married again. This marriage
and the birth of another son in 1865 inevitably made
a great difference to the boy's position at home, where
he had once been all-important. He resented the
change, and very soon father and son were nc longer
on their old footing of affectionate intimacy. In 1867
he was sent to a school near Berne, from which he

35

passed to Stuttgart, and this long absence did not mend
matters. Arthur complained of ungenerous treatment,
until at last he inherited some money from a grand-
aunt, after which he refused such help as Meredith
proffered from time to time. Without returning home,
he obtained work first at Havre and afterwards at
Lille, and began writing a little, several travel sketches
finding their way into *Macmillan's Magazine*. In 1881
he had serious trouble with his lungs, and Meredith,
on hearing of it, wrote at once offering help and suggesting that he should come home for a time. Arthur,
however, did not return and lived for a time in
Switzerland and Italy; but his health did not improve,
and at last, in 1889, he sailed for Australia. Feeling
somewhat improved by the voyage, he returned to
England, to his half-sister, Mrs. Clarke (the daughter
of Nicholls), at Woking, in the spring of 1890; but in
spite of careful nursing his condition grew worse, and
at the end of the summer he died. The tragedy of that
first marriage had worked itself out remorselessly, not
least in the scattered bright promise of this child of it
who had brought sorrow to both his parents. And in
the long estrangement of father from son, which the
son's obdurate pride had largely prevented from being
at last broken, history had repeated itself with a
vengeance.

We can now return to the literary chronicle. As
early as 1863, Meredith had planned a *picaresque* story
of the English roadside, in autobiographical form, to
be called *The Adventure of Richmond Roy and his
Friend, Contrivance Jack*. Eventually this story, now
differently planned though still retaining some *picaresque* elements, made its appearance as a serial in 1870

and 1871 in the *Cornhill Magazine* as *The Adventures of Harry Richmond*. It was published by Smith, Elder & Co. in three volumes, and attracted rather more notice than the previous novels. Meredith was still seeing a great deal of his friend Maxse, whom he had helped at Southampton during the election of 1868, when Maxse was a Radical candidate, and this friendship was to bear fruit in the novel on which Meredith was busily engaged during the years between 1871 and 1874. This was *Beauchamp's Career,* which was offered to the *Cornhill* and rejected, and eventually came out, in an abridged version, in the *Fortnightly Review* in 1874 and 1875. It was published in three volumes by Chapman & Hall, and in two volumes, for readers abroad, by Tauchnitz. The appearance of this novel, its author's favourite and undoubtedly one of his best performances, is generally held to be the turning-point in Meredith's career, the moment when he really found fame; but though the book was more widely and favourably noticed than any of the earlier ones, there is nothing in its reception to suggest that this particular novel marks the end of one phase and the beginning of another. If there has to be a turning-point, then it probably came with the succeeding novel, *The Egoist*.

During the two or three years following *Beauchamp's Career,* Meredith was chiefly occupied with poems and shorter prose things. In January 1877 the *New Quarterly Magazine* published his first short story (or short novel), *The House on the Beach,* an early work recently completed and a somewhat crude farcical affair. A month later he delivered his lecture *On the Idea of Comedy and the Uses of the Comic Spirit* at the London Institution, Finsbury Circus. It was really a reading of a carefully prepared essay, later published in the spring number of the *New Quarterly*, and it proved quite successful ("Audience very attentive and indulgent", as Meredith writes to Morley), though perhaps its greatest moment was when an Oriental, missing his way, marched into the room and stared about him. The summer number of this magazine also printed Meredith's little farcical story, *The Case of General Opie and Lady Camper,* which was partly based on an action by General Hopkins against his next-door neighbour, Lady Eleanor Cathcart, and was a reminiscence of Meredith's Kingston days. Two years later there appeared in the same magazine the third and by far the finest of his short stories, the exquisite *Tale of Chloe,* a little tragi-comedy of eighteenth-century Tunbridge Wells that has been singled out for special praise by some very good judges, but is still not as widely known and appreciated as it deserves to be. These three short tales remained for years inaccessible in book form, but now they make up a separate volume in the collected editions.

Meredith had by this time built his famous literary workshop, the chalet, on the high ground at the back of his garden. Here, ideally secluded, he produced *The Egoist,* actually begun in 1877 but not finished until February 1879. It is more than likely that the story was entirely rewritten, at least once, for we learn that it it was nearly completed in the summer of 1878, and yet in order to finish it when he did Meredith was compelled to work very hard at it for the last three months, writing far into the night. His subsequent ill-health has been considered partly as the legacy of this period of nervous strain and exhaustion. The book was published in three volumes by Kegan, Paul & Co. in the autumn of 1879. The publishers, without consulting Meredith, sold the serial rights to the *Glasgow Weekly Herald,* where it appeared (surely the oddest of all *feuilletons*) as *Sir Willoughby Patterne, the Egoist.* Ironically enough, Meredith, after mentioning the novel to Stevenson in a letter, remarks: "I don't think you will like it: I doubt if those who care for my work will take to it at all. And for this reason, after doing my best with it, I am in no hurry to see it appear. It is a Comedy, with only half of me in it, unlikely therefore to take either the public or my friends." The irony lies in the fact that this novel, above all others, widened and strengthened his reputation, and the correspondent "who will not like it" was one of the foremost persons instrumental in spreading the fame of the book and its author. Meredith must have been writing out of that fit of doubt and slight depression which so frequently follows the short-lived joy of having completed a piece of work. Moreover, having been disappointed so many times, the novelist was determined to expect little or nothing in the way of appreciation. But once more he was doomed to disappointment, this time pleasantly, for *The Egoist* was an undoubted success. The leading newspapers and weekly reviews, with Henley and others spurring them on, hastened to welcome it with the warmest praise. A second edition in one volume was brought out within the year. This may not seem very impressive, in these days of unlimited editions, but it is as well to remember that it was far more

difficult to dispose of one edition of a three-volume
novel (costing about thirty shillings) than it is now
to sell three or four editions of single volumes at six
shillings or seven-and-sixpence. Meredith had now
consolidated his position. Articles on his work were
frequent, and most of the brilliant young men of
the time were his enthusiastic admirers. Oxford and
Cambridge, as we are told, "were all madly in love
with him". No longer could he reasonably complain,
though he did complain to the end of his life, of being
neglected and unappreciated. The general reading public may have still lagged behind, but to the intellectuals,
the companies of "warm young men", he became more
than a writer, he became a cult, and Box Hill an
Olympus.

The 'seventies and the early 'eighties were years
rich in friendship for Meredith, for most of his older
friends were still alive and in touch with him, and every
year brought him new ones, particularly among the
younger men of letters. A most fruitful literary
friendship was brought about by an early meeting with
Stevenson, who, with his friend Henley, did much to
trumpet abroad the novelist's genius. James Thomson,
the unhappy "B. V.", wrote appreciations and paid
visits to Flint Cottage, and so did Grant Allen and,
later, J. M. Barrie. John Morley was a frequent
visitor and correspondent. Another notable friend
was Leslie Stephen, whose scholarship and pedestrian
powers and long lean frame suggested to Meredith
his "Phoebus Apollo turned fasting friar", Vernon
Whitford in *The Egoist*. The year that first saw this
novel also saw the foundation, by Stephen, of the
Sunday Tramps, a group of friends, Sir Frederick

Pollock, John Collier, R. B. Haldane, D. MacColl, and others, who, under the leadership of Stephen, spent their Sundays tramping the countryside in Surrey and Kent. These genial and learned pedestrians frequently found themselves in the neighbourhood of Box Hill, where they would be met by Meredith and entertained at Flint Cottage. On one occasion, mentioned both by Meredith in a letter and by Stephen in an article, the Tramps picnicked on Leith Hill on hock and cold sausages conveyed from Flint Cottage in a knapsack. Stephen and Meredith were close friends to the end, and when both were aged and feeble, Stephen actually dying, they exchanged pathetic letters wistfully recalling their old powers. But even in the early 'eighties Meredith's days as a walker were numbered. After finishing *The Egoist* he paid a visit to France, only to find that his health became worse on his return to this country. Within a year or so his deranged digestion brought about further trouble, and very soon movement began to be difficult. "As I am unpopular", he writes to his son Arthur in 1881, "I am ill-paid, and therefore bound to work double tides, hardly ever able to lay down the pen. This affects my weakened stomach, and so the round of the vicious circle is looped."

In spite of ill-health, however, he produced *The Tragic Comedians* in an amazingly short space of time, and it was published at the end of 1880. An abridged form had appeared in the *Fortnightly Review,* and not long after the appearance of the two-volume edition it found its way into a popular two-shilling series by Ward, Lock. But this curious novel, if it can be called a novel, for it follows the actual story of Ferdinand

Lassalle and Hélène von Dönniges very closely and is perhaps best regarded as one of a new species, a cross between history or biography and fiction, has never found much favour even among Meredith's admirers. It shows very plainly the marks of hasty writing and construction, and the story is too huddled. But it has great force and drive, and in spite of obvious weaknesses *The Tragic Comedians* has probably been just as greatly underestimated as its successor, *Diana of the Crossways,* has been overestimated. Before completing *Diana,* however, Meredith turned to poetry again, and in 1883 brought out, with Macmillan, his *Poems and Lyrics of the Joy of Earth.* This volume undoubtedly contains his finest verse, including "The Woods of Westermain", the revised version of "Love in the Valley", "The Lark Ascending", and the three poems on classical themes, "The Day of the Daughter of Hades", "Phoebus with Admetus", and "Melampus". No other single volume of his can show us so much rich treasure of thought and imagery.

A year later twenty-six chapters of *Diana* made their appearance in the *Fortnightly,* and the whole story, in three volumes, was published at the beginning of 1885. It is based, of course, on the history of Mrs. Caroline Norton, whose acquaintance Meredith had made at the Duff Gordons' many years before. Unfortunately he made use of a story, which accused Mrs. Norton of betraying a political secret to *The Times,* that had no basis in fact, the actual culprit being Lord Aberdeen, with the result that her relative, Lord Dufferin and Ava. was greatly offended, and some pressure was brought to bear on the novelist to deny the truth of the legend he had helped to circulate. That is why later editions of the book were prefaced by a note stating that the story should be read as fiction. *Diana of the Crossways* was far more successful than any of its predecessors. The critics were fascinated by Diana herself, and the faintly scandalous interest of the book attracted a wider public than that which had read and enjoyed the earlier novels. It is, however, not easy to explain why this novel should occupy the position it does, as the most popular and widely known of all Meredith's novels, for compared with such things as *Evan Harrington* and *Harry Richmond*, filled as they are with romantic incident and delightful comedy, *Diana of the Crossways* is obscure and baffling and far less likely, one would have thought, to have attracted a public that left the earlier novels unread.

The tragic irony that seems to run all through Meredith's life makes its appearance again, for on top of this first undoubted literary success of his there came crashing a blow that left him indifferent to the praise and blame of critics and the patronage of library subscribers. In February 1885, Mrs. Meredith, who had not been well for some time, was compelled to have an operation. She was removed to Eastbourne for a time but made little progress, and finally came back to Box Hill in June, a dying woman, lingering on until the middle of September. She was buried in Dorking Cemetery. In his grief, Meredith, who was always a poet at heart and always preferred to be thought one, turned to poetry. "A Faith on Trial", "Change in Recurrence", and other poems of this period were plainly written in the shadow of this loss. Two volumes of verse followed one another in fairly quick succession, *Ballads and Poems of Tragic Life,* which contains nothing of great moment, and the more important *A Reading of Earth,* both published by Macmillan. The next few years, with some intervals for travel, notably in Cornwall and Wales (where his son was studying as an electrical engineer), were occupied in writing the poems that subsequently appeared in "The Empty Purse", published by Macmillan in 1892, and the novel *One of our Conquerors.*

This story was serialised simultaneously in England, America, and Australia, notwithstanding the fact that it is generally held to be the most difficult and teasing of all Meredith's novels. Years later, he told M. Photiadès, who is the author of a critical study of the novelist, that having inherited a small sum of money and feeling independent, he determined to serve the critics with what he called "a strong dose of my most indigestible production", of which the introductory chapters of *One of our Conquerors* are perhaps the best example. If this statement is strictly true, if Meredith did deliberately make his later work obscure, then he ought to have been ashamed of himself. Authorship is not a standing feud with a few indolent or hostile reviewers, and a writer ought to have other things in his mind, when he is planning and executing a piece of work, than the opportunity it presents of paying off a few old scores. But we may very well doubt if Meredith's statement was strictly true. By that time he realised that during the early 'nineties he had become the victim of a mannerism that made his work, both in verse and prose, increasingly crabbed and obscure. Instead of admitting the weakness, which had been made plain to him by criticism (to which he was not indifferent, as he pretended, far from it), he chose to explain it away by confessing that it was deliberate on his part. Either way, Meredith does not come out of the affair very well.

In 1893 *Lord Ormont and his Aminta* began a serial appearance in the *Pall Mall Magazine,* and was published by Chapman & Hall in the summer of 1894. It was the last of Meredith's novels to appear in the now unfamiliar three-volume form, for which there is more to be said than most people imagine, as it did at least enable authors to write stories of some length without considerable loss of money. On the heels of *Lord Ormont and his Aminta* came *The Amazing Marriage,* a story that had been begun fifteen years before. It was taken up and completed at the suggestion of the friend whose name figures in the dedication. An abridged version was published as a serial by *Scribner's Magazine,* and in the same year, 1895, the novel itself was brought out by Constable & Co., in which firm the novelist's son, Mr. William Maxse Meredith, was now working. The character of Gower Woodseer, in the earlier but not the later chapters of *The Amazing Marriage,* was based on the figure of the youthful Stevenson, who used to visit Flint Cottage in the later 'seventies, Stevenson himself dying just before the story made its appearance in *Scribner's.* This was the last novel Meredith completed. After his death, an earlier unfinished story, *Celt and Saxon,* of some though not very great promise, was published. Another and perhaps more interesting fragment, of a very much earlier period, may be found in the volume devoted to Miscellaneous Prose in the Collected Edition. This is *The Gentleman of Fifty and the Damsel of Nineteen,* a story related in the first person by these two respective characters in alternate chapters, and marked by an unusually simple and direct manner and style. The five chapters remaining to us foreshadow a very pleasant romantic comedy and constitute Meredith's most tantalising and promising fragment. Another unfinished work was the idyllic comedy *The Sentimentalists,* which might be shortly described as fine phrases in a garden. A version edited by Sir James Barrie and produced by Mr. Granville Barker found its way into the programme of the Repertory Season at the Duke of York's Theatre in 1910.

This completes the table of Meredith's prose, but he had not yet finished with his novels. The first Uniform Edition of the novels was brought out by Chapman & Hall in the years 1885-1887, and was reprinted, with additions, in 1889. In 1896 Constable & Co. began to issue *The Works of George Meredith* in 36 volumes, and for this splendid edition Meredith decided to revise his earlier novels, in particular *The Ordeal of Richard Feverel* and *Evan Harrington,* from which long passages, sometimes whole chapters (the original first four chapters of *Richard Feverel* being condensed into one), were excised. Far too much fuss has been made about this revision. So many critics have exclaimed against it and have advised their readers to obtain *The Ordeal of Richard Feverel* and *Evan Harrington* in the original versions, that such readers might very well be excused if they imagined that the more recent editions defrauded them of whole chapters of the highest wit and poetry. Actually they are only missing a few very readable and, for the most part, rather farcical passages of no great importance to the stories that once contained them. It has been said that the story of the Feverels cannot be fully understood now that most of the explanatory matter at the beginning has been cut out. This is not true, as everything necessary can be found in the first chapter, the other, excised, chapters only commenting at unnecessary length on Sir Austin Feverel's attitude of mind towards Woman and other matters at Raynham Abbey, with a broad touch of caricature rather foreign to the character of the story. There is actually little to choose between the original and the revised versions; if the latter lose a few high-spirited passages, they also gain in condensation and unity.

His prose work was done, but he still continued writing poetry, of which there were three more volumes to come. The first was *Odes in Contribution to the Song of French History,* published in 1898 and dedicated to John Morley. Three years later came *A Reading of Life,* consisting of poems that had been contributed to various periodicals, and then after his death the final gleaning, *Last Poems.* Meanwhile, of course, his earlier poetry had been reprinted in various forms. There is not much to record of the last fifteen years of his life. The paralysis that had set in after his first serious illness became more pronounced as time went on, and to it was added deafness, but he contrived to retain a youthfulnes of spirit that nothing could wither. He rarely stayed away from his cottage for long, but friends and admirers frequently called upon him. Indeed, the pilgrimage to Box Hill seems to have been a marked feature of the literary life of this country during the years 1895-1909. His position was now assured, and though he complained to the end of a lack of appreciation, it is not easy to understand where he found it, for his old age was crowded with honours. On the death of Tennyson, in 1892, he was chosen as President of the Society of Authors. Six years later, on his seventieth birthday, he was presented with an address of congratulation signed by a number of his fellow-authors. During the Boer War he added the weight of his reputation and years to the party who opposed the war, and, at its conclusion, wrote several letters to the Press pleading for better treatment of the Boers. A year later he had the misfortune to fall and break his leg. But though only able to move about in a bath-chair he still sought the open air, and every day might be seen between Flint Cottage and the summit of Box Hill, being drawn in his bath-chair by his donkey "Picnic". In 1905 he accepted the Order of Merit. Three years later, on the 12th of February 1908, he celebrated his eightieth birthday and received various congratulatory addresses. For a week or so he was the darling of the Press, which published innumerable photographs, interviews, and eulogistic articles. On these late celebrations Meredith cast a somewhat sardonic eye and refused to change his opinion of his own standing, remarking to a visitor, "Certainly at this late hour they accord me a little glory; my name is famous, but no one reads my books". His eighty-first birthday still found him alert in mind, ready to receive the few old friends who came to call on him; but in May, going out for his usual drive, he caught a chill, took to his bed, and died in the early morning of May 18, 1909. He is buried beside his wife in Dorking Cemetery in the very heart of his beloved Surrey countryside whose hills and woods and heaths had given him the scene of so many stories and the burden of so many songs.

Meredith's chief characteristic, as all his friends and acquaintances testify, was an immense vitality. He was tremendously alive, both physically and mentally. In order to understand what he was in the prime of life, we have to forget the photographs with which we are all familiar, the delicate-looking, finely-cut profile of his old age, and turn to such records as remain of his earlier days, when he was for ever in the open, a poet and an athlete, a wit on the march, an erect, broad-shouldered figure, with a manly, handsome, mobile face, a creature at once strong and nervous, like a racehorse. He had a great and memorable laugh and a somewhat loud and drawling voice, though once free from any touch of self-consciousness he talked at great speed. As a talker he was famous. Many good judges have held that he was the finest talker of his time, and even those, and they are not wanting, who considered him affected in speech, too anxious to impress, too assiduous in his search for the epigrammatic phrase, have not denied the force and brilliance of his talk. Like most men of his type, he was not a conversationalist so much as a monologuist, and this tendency to talk most of the time himself, merely making his companion's remarks the stage for a new flight, would naturally grow stronger with the advent of years and fame. It is well to remember, however, that for one account of him as a talker from some boon companion of his earlier or middle years, we have fifty from later admirers, who were there not to talk but merely to lend an ear to the great man's discourse. Later in life he was bathed in a not altogether healthy atmosphere of prostrate adoration and gush (it is curious that a man whose work has so little of it should have received so much gush), and being a man by no means without vanity, who put immense self-knowledge and devastating humour into his work, but was apt to leave it out of his life, he took care to live up to the demands made upon him. He was expected to talk for show, and so he talked for show.

Earlier records present us with an equally brilliant but a much more companionable person. H. M. Hyndman, for example, tells us how, as an undergraduate in the early 'sixties, he spent a few days with Meredith and several of his close friends at Seaford. "Meredith in particular", he remarks, "was at his best in those days, and being quite at home with the men around him, and with no audience he felt it incumbent upon him to dazzle, and waiting to appreciate his good things, he delivered himself without effort or artifice of all the really profound and poetic and humorous thoughts on men and things that welled continually within him in a manner that I recall with delight these long years afterwards." It was during his stay at Seaford that Burnand, who, notwithstanding the fact that he was an old friend of Meredith's, always confessed that he had found the later novels completely unreadable, suddenly broke in with "Damn you, George; why don't you write as you talk?" His talk, like his best writing, had an immense range, and was crammed with wit and observation, poetry and humour. He had a trick, common to most of the best literary talkers, of allowing his humorous fancy to go soaring into the very blue of absurdity, sometimes, as one of his friends relates, raising an account of the life and character of an acquaintance into a monstrously comic and entirely imaginary biography, in which, however, truth to character would be preserved to the very end. Like Dickens, he lived intimately with the chief personages of his novels, having imagined them intensely, and would talk of them as if they were real people.

Some of his literary high spirits find their way into his letters, particularly the early ones to such friends as Hardman, which are alive with good-fellowship, pleasant fooling, and helter-skelter rhyming. But his letters as a whole are very disappointing. They lack the supreme quality of charm. Too frequently they are written in what we might call the Meredithian grand manner, and are self-conscious, didactic, stilted. There is to be heard in them a certain tone of voice (and many of his characters have it), dogmatic and authoritative, clipped and vaguely insolent, which to most of us is extremely irritating and entirely unfit for ordinary reasonable human intercourse. There are of course many good things in the letters, flashes of real wisdom, occasional touches of poetry, and here and there some very acute criticism of men and books, but as a whole they are too obviously lacking in the essential qualities of sympathy and charm, the friendly smile looking out of the page, to be worth a place in even the third or fourth rank of Letters. The very worst of his novels can afford to look down on his letters, and can, indeed, reveal to us far more of the man who penned them.

So far, no close examination and analysis of Meredith's character has been attempted by any of his biographers and critics. It is not difficult to see why. He lived in a great age, and most studies of his work and sketches of his life and personality were produced during his lifetime, and were indeed written by enthusiastic admirers under his very eye, as it were, and with his blessing. Under these circumstances it is not possible to do anything more than hint at fault. When at last he did die, a splendid figure in himself and the last representative of a great period, there followed, on the heels of the customary chorus of panegyrics, the natural reaction, the silence that indicates that criticism wishes to change the subject. The biography of Mr. S. M. Ellis, which provides us with a number of facts hitherto unknown to the general public, broke that silence, but it only gives us the material and does not pretend to be a psychological study. That has still to come, and no doubt it will come, for Meredith was unquestionably a fascinating subject. Meanwhile a comparatively short critical study of this kind is no place in which to attempt a close examination of his character, but something must be said of it, if only because a complete understanding of his work is not possible unless some attempt is made to understand the man himself. It will possibly have been remarked that people who are faced with the personality of Meredith are either dazzled or are hostile. Even the persons who are hostile are dazzled, but they dislike the condition and mistrust the man responsible for it. They have departed, cherishing a vague notion that the god had feet of clay.

At first sight, the figure of Meredith is so splendid, so rich in qualities, rarely combined in one man, that criticism is silent. The writer has faults plain for the world to see, but the man himself flashes by, a radiant creature, reminding us of those magnificent beings of the Renaissance. We always discover him at the

height of his powers, ready, composed, pouring out
poetry, wit, acute criticism of his fellow-creatures; we
never come upon him in a weak and unguarded
moment, never catch him depressed, bewildered,
contrite; he is always present in his full force. It is
an impressive spectacle. But if we have spent any
time in the company, though it is only in our library,
of great men of letters, particularly such men as
Johnson and Fielding, Lamb and Thackeray and
Carlyle, we cannot help feeling that the sight is a
little too impressive, that the complete absence of those
unguarded moments is in itself suspicious, that
Meredith is always, as it were, on show. And then,
when we refuse merely to gape, but turn upon him
those searchlights that he turned upon his own
creatures, surveying coldly those facts that are now
made known to us, there is a moment when the idol
seems to have crashed down in ruins at our feet. The
faults of all his victims seem to be gathered together
in the person of their creator. Not one of his ironic
comedies appears so searching and merciless as this
ironic comedy of his own life. Here is a man who
concerns himself with the delicate adjustment of
human relationships and yet contrives, before he
has finished, to quarrel bitterly with his father, his
wife, and his son. He may possibly have been in the
right, or had more justice on his side, in each of these
quarrels, but the melancholy sequence itself is suspicious. Here, too, is a man who has made himself the
spokesman of a rigid intellectual honesty and sincerity,
and yet does not shrink from writing for years on what
was incontestably for him the wrong side. Here is
the pitiless satirist, the unsparing opponent of social

vanities, hypocrisies, and snobberies, who to the very end of his life, as we have seen, would seem to have wished to conceal the facts of his origin.

There are times when he seems as deeply dyed in cold egoism as his own Sir Willoughby Patterne. And there was in him, it would almost seem, something implacable; he could not forgive an injury, nor even forget a fancied slight, and fancied slights were very common in his history. Even his early benefactors, it would seem, did not always escape his resentment, and he usually contrived to have for them more hard words than gratitude. It is significant that when the editor who printed his first attempts in verse wrote to him years afterwards, reminding him of the fact and suggesting a meeting, no reply was forthcoming from Meredith. One of the friends of his later years, Lady Butcher, has told us how his pride made him dislike receiving even the smallest presents, and, facing the not uncommon charge of ingratitude against Meredith, has pointed out to us that "no one should expect an eagle to be grateful". With eagles we have nothing to do, but the pride that forbids the expression of ordinary gratitude is not the mark of a great mind but a little one. There is about great men a certain almost careless magnanimity, a large and easy tolerance, the attitude of a good-humoured giant among creatures of a lesser stature, that enables them to wave away the smaller injuries and grievances and to deal gently with old opponents. They have large reserves of strength and do not need to tighten themselves up for every casual encounter. They act in such a way that they can be appreciated as men, and there is no necessity to excuse them as eagles. This plain human dignity in the more important concerns of life and this lounging good-humour in the more trifling affairs are both absent from Meredith. To make a not uncommon distinction, he was a great writer, but he was not a great man.

The secret of his weakness is of course pride, something colder and harder and infinitely more dangerous than the eager soaring vanity that distinguishes so many artists. Meredith may have been vain; he probably was, just as Goldsmith and Stevenson and scores of other delightful and lovable writers were vain; but he was something more. In his life, though not in his work, he was proud and egoistical. It was this pride that impelled him into those hot quarrels with those about him, and, what was far worse, prevented him from making the easy gesture that might have put an end to them. It was pride that kept him resenting not only injuries, fancied or otherwise, but even the existence of former benefactors. Nearly every fault can be traced to this source. And it is possible to dig underneath it to what was lying below. His upbringing, as we have seen, was not altogether fortunate. He was an only child, ultra-sensitive, precocious, in a house of adults, a child taught to think himself the superior of the children in the immediate vicinity, the son of an anxious and for ever wincing genteel tailordom. There was elaborate self-deception in the very air. He grew up, a brilliant, ambitious, sensitive youth, who resented what he considered his ridiculous social background (the real thrust being, as we can see from *Evan Harrington,* not so much that his family were tradespeople as that they were *tailors,* those time-honoured butts of the cheap wit; his schooldays had probably taught him what could be made out of this fact), who further resented his poverty, and, later, the neglect from which his work suffered for so long. He became morbidly sensitive.

A highly-strung, taut, amazingly impressionable, lightning-witted creature, for ever wincing at the lightest word, felled by the lifting of an eyebrow, carrying with him so many secrets that were almost ludicrous and shameful, knowing himself to be an original artist with his way, and a very rough way, to make, yet feeling all the time that he was something of a mere adventurer, Meredith did what many persons of a like temper have done, he made for himself a suit of armour. The naked man went into his work, which is itself largely an attack upon armour. The haughty, dogmatic, supremely self-confident Olympian who passed as George Meredith was not the real man at all. He was—as those who like him least would be compelled to admit—an original creative artist and a good deal of an original thinker, an innovator in more ways than one, but he had not the toughness that usually accompanies such originality and serves as a protection for its possessor. His almost aggressively self-confident manner, like that of many other sensitive persons, was a mere mask through which there peered a taut and anxious self. He was a man for ever in the midst of battle, tightly strung up, and so he could not afford to be tolerant and easy. Had he really been half so self-assured as he pretended to be, he could have been more careless, more good-humoured, but he could no more allow himself such indulgence than Richmond Roy could afford to relax his social vigilance. Few writers have pretended to be more indifferent to criticism than Meredith, and it is doubtful if there ever was a writer more sensitive to it. Hostile criticism did him a great deal of harm, because when it passed over the good things in his work as well as censuring the real weaknesses, he deliberately hardened his heart against it, and instead of modifying his mannerisms, flung them in the critics' faces. A man who was genuinely indifferent to critical opinion would have gone quietly on his way, but Meredith was always working self-consciously, seeing, as it were, the critical eye upon him and, if it were not a friendly eye (he was greatly influenced by the opinion of his close friends), steeling himself to flout it. All his references to criticism and the reviewers, to his own position in the literary world, point to an extreme sensitiveness and self-consciousness.

Nor were the circumstances of his literary career favourable for his relieving himself of this armour, for a return to a more naked sincerity. He found himself confronted by a vast apathy not entirely unmixed with actual hostility, which in turn caused his ever-increasing band of admirers to assume attitudes of sheer prostration. He became an oracle. His name became a battle-cry. The George Meredith he had in a measure invented, now became not only his, but other people's George Meredith. This was no time for casting off his armour, and so, before he had done, that armour had, as it were, grown on him like a skin. Had his literary history been different, had he been quietly and naturally accepted, praised for his great qualities, and gently chided for his faults, the sequel would have been very different, but, as it was, everything conspired to raise the doubtful seed sown during his childhood into a sturdy growth, robbing him, who would seem to have had all the virtues, of the greatest and noblest virtue, charity.

We have already surprised what is perhaps the secret of Meredith, having, indeed, begun his history with a note upon it, and we shall have to dwell upon it more than once in what follows. Put in paradoxical shape, it is that he was a great writer because he was not a great man. His strength as a creator and a critic of life lay in his very weakness as a man. And since, in the last resort, this distinction between the writer and the man will not hold, as the writer *is* the man, and the man is never more himself than when he is actually creating, we cannot dismiss the subject of his character without some reference to his work. The snobbish pride that may have led him to conceal his birth, he flayed alive in *Evan Harrington*. He may have shown himself somewhat unfeeling in his last relations with his first wife, but he could give us "Modern Love" with all its insight and tenderness and charity. He may possibly have been his own hero in his life, but he is never his own hero in his works, which celebrate other and very different kinds of men and only turn to persons in whom there is some weakness of his own when they have sharpened the sword and pointed the arrows. Such faults as he had are there, transfixed for ever, in his memorable comedies, which remain with us as his apology when we should think such apology necessary. The very criticism that discovers his weaknesses has been made more sensitive and strengthened by his own hand.

CHAPTER III

HIS ATTITUDE: NATURE—MAN—EARTH

In their studies of the more important literary figures, critics usually examine and comment upon the actual work first and then contrive to wring from it an amount of "philosophy" or "teaching" sufficient to fill a final chapter, whose easy rhetoric is commonly nothing more than a huge sigh of relief. It is an agreeable method, but it has one disadvantage, for it tends to throw the emphasis not upon the work itself, but upon this "philosophy" or "teaching", this matter for the final chapter. Thus it would often seem that the critic, by writing his final chapter, had done all that the author in question intended to do when he wrote his volumes of poetry or fiction, and having done it, having distilled the didactic essence from the poems and novels in a score or so pages, had therefore done it better. This is clearly absurd. The greatest legacy a writer can leave us is obviously not the body of doctrine that may be deduced from his poetry or his fiction, but the actual poems and novels themselves. If we can appreciate them to the full extent of our powers, then we shall have ready to hand all the writer's philosophy and a great deal more besides, everything, in short, he can give us. Even with

Meredith, one of the most didactic and philosophical of poets and novelists, this familiar method cannot be safely employed, if our business is literary criticism, so that it is more profitable to examine his attitude first and his work afterwards. It is true that his poems and his novels are the vehicles of his philosophy, and therefore we are compelled to read them before we can understand what his attitude is; but his work is at once so rich and complex that we can only enjoy it to the full once we have grasped the attitude of mind underlying it. This is particularly true of the fiction which supplies us with endless and very subtle variations on themes directly stated by the poetry. The notion, popularised by well-meaning but foolish admirers of Meredith, that his fiction must be approached only after prayers and fasting and solemn ceremonies of initiation, is a very ridiculous one and has turned away thousands of plain sensible readers from these novels. In spite of numerous defects they can be enjoyed at once by anybody who can sit at the table of letters and has not to be spoon-fed, for whatever else these novels may be, they are certainly a rich feast of story-telling. Nevertheless, it is true to say that the better novels, and particularly *The Egoist*, will be enjoyed more at a third or fourth reading, when the reader is in possession of certain philosophical clues, when the novelist's attitude of mind is made plain, when the reader is acquainted with the theme, and can settle down to enjoy the variations. The plainest statement of such themes is to be found in the poetry. In his poetry Meredith is the god oracular, showering down precepts and aphorisms from the blue. In his fiction he is the god in action, moving invisibly among men, nerving an arm here, directing a shaft there, and bringing to pass the doom he has foretold as oracle.

Meredith is one of the few poets and novelists who can claim a body of opinion and beliefs worthy to be called "philosophy", a word that was frequently passing his own lips and is never long absent from the pages of his critics. His claim is so good that he is entitled to a very definite place in any extensive history of English Thought, and already he has made an appearance in several such histories. But the term "philosophy" has its dangers. It suggests something more systematic and reasoned, less intuitional and fragmentary, than anything that Meredith can offer us. Faced with a "philosophy", we are apt to become exacting. We demand cosmological grandeur, a whole universe taken to pieces and put together again; we grow contemptuous at the sight of empty spaces and loose ends; we wish to place it among one of the existing "isms" or require that it shall form a new "ism". We are not to be put off with mingled gleams of wit and poetry, the smouldering and flashing oracle in place of the slow and toiling sage. It would be difficult to find a man less like the professional philosopher than Meredith, who took no pleasure in accumulating evidence, in adding instance to instance, in weighing and balancing and exact recording. His wits were gunpowder, and his mind worked in magnificent flashes, spluttering and crackling on its way, like a burning fuse, from one explosion of humour and high emotion to another. He is never caught on the way, but is always at the end of an intellectual journey. He can make great play with his conclusions about life, twisting them this way and that, making them the basis of a song, a sheaf of aphorisms, an elaborate narrative, but what he does not do is to show us how he arrived at them. His method and manner are always the oracular. Therefore it will be better to abandon the term "philosophy", which would only invite a kind of criticism that his beliefs were never intended to meet, and to talk instead of his "attitude". If we examine his beliefs and opinions as an attitude, we shall then be surprised to discover how coherent and systematic they appear to be.

The first thing to be noted about this attitude is the curious way in which it seems to escape the age in which he lived. Meredith, we may say, is *in* but not *of* the nineteenth century. He looks forward and backward. In some respects he clearly looks back to the eighteenth century, whose wits and fine ladies and gentlemen, whose social sanity, whose grave impertinences masking unruffled good sense, stir again in his narratives. Take Meredith indoors and set the wine before him, and it seems as if the nineteenth century has not yet begun. Yet in other respects—and these have not been sufficiently noticed—it is obvious that he looks forward to our own century, which arrived when he was past seventy. He is still ahead of most of our contemporaries. At the present time, when Meredith is in danger of serious neglect, perhaps in greater danger than most of the more important writers of his time, it is precisely *his* ideas that are slowly permeating the mass of cultivated opinion. Half the new ideas of last year can be found, admirably condensed, thrown off like sparks from the grindstone, in some little lyric or other that Meredith wrote fifty or sixty years ago. He, almost alone of his generation, does not "date", and persons who imagine that he does are ignorant either of his work or of the progress of thought. Meredith's head and shoulders are still too broad to be squeezed into any of those Victorian frames that we gild so lavishly with our post-War irony. No bland references to the Albert Memorial or *The Idylls of the King* or the Great Exhibition or the Jubilee can reduce Meredith to a posturing bewhiskered pigmy, a toy lion. He escapes from his age so completely that at times only chronology can reassure us.

There are many reasons for this curious escape, and they are concerned not merely with the nature of his beliefs, but also with the manner in which they are held. Meredith is extraordinarily free from that sense of strain which accompanies so many great Victorian writers and thinkers. Where most of his great contemporaries seem lop-sided and strained, as if they had been compelled to cut off an arm or a leg to save the rest of the intellectual body (which is precisely what they had to do), he is at once complete, compact and buoyant, and his attitude is, as it were, all of a piece. We do not encounter him groaning to achieve some kind of synthesis: he springs out upon us an Athene, fully grown and fully armed. The great Victorians, as Mr. Chesterton once pointed out, are nearly all curiously lop-sided. They grew to maturity at a time when one set of ideas, familiar, warm, comforting, were being rudely challenged and assailed by another set of ideas, new, disturbing, and not easily set aside. Science, attended by a regiment of prancing "isms", took the field against Religion, and the thoughtful Victorian had to side with one or the other, or had to try, in the teeth of their mutual defiance, to reconcile them. It is true that a new set of ideas is always challenging an old set, and in view of the fact that the air is still ringing with such challenges, it may be thought that too much has been made of this old quarrel. But it was the first real crash, and it was the greatest, not because the questions at issue were necessarily any more significant than those of a later date, but, from our present point of view, because of its effect.

The Victorians had been educated to believe, their minds were formed to hold some faith very strongly, and so they were compelled to make a choice. The human mind, after a time, reacts to an environment of whirling and contesting ideas much as the human body, if time is allowed it, reacts to a microbe-laden atmosphere, in short, it adapts itself to the new conditions. Men begin to grasp ideas rather more lightly; the old earnestness disappears and the necessity of holding some fixed set of beliefs soon seems less pressing; and various shades of scepticism, smoked glasses for the mind's eye, soon make their appearance. This automatically protective and comfortable adaptation has been long in progress, but it had hardly begun eighty years ago. Men had to be earnest believers in something, if only in "honest doubt"; they had to make a choice and were so situated that, in choosing, it seemed inevitable that something valuable was always lost, sacrificed on the altar of logical necessity, and for this reason there was about so many of them a certain sense of strain. If they lose hold of our sympathies even for a moment, they begin to turn into caricatures of themselves and titillate our sense of humour: we catch sight of them clenching their fists and grinding their teeth in the act of doubting or believing; or we see them deliberately putting a patch over one eye and staring straight ahead with the remaining one, commenting all the while, with almost pathetic eagerness, on the breadth and fullness of the landscape. Dickens, being simply a child of genius, escapes by never entering into a world of ideas. Thackeray, dubious and uneasy, takes refuge in his club, and rowning in the purely dramatic and grotesque, and when these fail him, falls back on mere romantic heartiness. All these escape in a measure, but a sense of strain and a certain lopsidedness are very evident in the others. Tennyson, nothing if not conscientious, groans over some sounding lines on honest doubt and the creeds, and plainly wishes it were time to return to strange shadowy landscapes and elfin twilights. Carlyle leaves us doubtful whether we are being treated to a baffled and indignant idealism or to chronic dyspepsia. George Eliot, after the most strenuous efforts, can only ask us to "do without opium and live through all our pain", and has obviously found so little satisfaction in the process that we are tempted to send out for opium at once. John Stuart Mill methodically reduces the universe to a convenient size and shape, and ever afterwards finds himself a little wistful; a man haunted by a faintly remembered sweet singing, by the ghost of a murdered poet. Newman sharpens his intellect and hacks it almost to pieces in the attempt to prove that it is not to be trusted. Matthew Arnold retires delicately to the wilderness to coin a phrase, the "something not ourselves which makes for righteousness", conjures it into a private deity, and thereafter coins no more phrases. Jowett, after a short struggle, trots away from it all and very blandly combines the worship of Plato with the worship of success. Clough suffers and doubts and doubts and suffers until there seems nothing left for him but either a little intellectual dishonesty or drink. On each side of these thinkers, the elect, are the crowds of extremists, the clergymen who live in universes like toy farms, and the materialists who live in universes like colossal steam-engines. And from all this Meredith escaped.

Actually, of course, his ideas must have a history, and if we pressed him very closely, we should discover that his body of opinions does not differ very much from those of his philosophical Radical friends of the mid-century. They have a threefold basis of naturalism, positivism, and radicalism. And in some respects, we can observe actual influences that can be given a date at work in his mind. Thus he was arriving at maturity when the sun of 1848 burst upon the world and ripened innumerable crops of revolution; and to the last, in his political thinking, Meredith still seems to breathe the heady air of 1848. His radicalism has a militant nationalistic temper to the very last, and if we observe him closely, beneath his apparent detachment and occasional little cynicisms we can hear faint echoes of Mazzini's burning rhetoric and catch a fleeting glimpse of Kossuth and his broken legions. That sun of 1848 never quite set in Meredith's mind, and it warmed him through all the years of disillusion and the cold prophesying of economists. It would, then, be an error to imagine him entirely timeless, without a background; and yet, compared with his contemporaries, that is precisely what he suggests to us. The fact that, with him, there seems to be no struggle, no desperate sacrifice of something valuable, no consequent strain, may mean that he was wiser than his contemporaries or that he was more foolish; that he saw further than they did and was able to achieve a kind of synthesis without effort; or that he did not see as far, had blind spots, and so never saw that a sacrifice had been made. But that fact remains. It would seem as if a temperament, an education (for had Meredith gone to Arnold's Rugby and then to Oxford, we should have had a different tale to tell), and a set of ideas all met together and found themselves perfectly adjusted to one another.

Meredith escapes the Science-Religion, materialism-idealism trap because he is by temperament something different from all his contemporaries; he is a pure pagan. Other literary men of the century are often considered pagans when they are really nothing but occasional blasphemers, pretending to worship Lucifer or to celebrate the black mass on occasion. Poets like Byron and Swinburne, for example, are nothing but naughty little boys peeping round the church door and making faces at the parson. They still live in a Christian world, even though they may at times go swaggering through it as friends of the devil. But Meredith, from the first, does not seem to live at all in the universe of Christian theology. One feels with him that if Evolution had not been there he would have had to invent it. This marks the difference between him and his contemporaries. To them Evolution was a black draught that had either to be gulped down or spat out, and whether they drank it or rejected it, they were always uneasy about Nature. We catch sight of them, as it were, hurrying indoors at the earliest possible moment. That is why so many of them seem to live in a gas-lit shuttered universe, and why with Meredith, who appeared to take Evolution in his stride and was never happy unless he was talking about Nature, we feel that the sun is shining and the great winds blowing for the first time in Victorian literature. And like most mental attitudes remarkable for their unity (though not for a strictly logical unity), Meredith's attitude contains a number of apparent contradictions. Thus, he is a born optimist, epicurean in temperament, who holds what is at bottom a stoical creed. He is a naturalistic philosopher whose every naturalistic fact has somehow a mystical glow. He is a poetic and witty radical of a marked aristocratic temper. Everywhere he really occupies a middle position, believes in temperance, balance, and the nothing too much (the "inspired prophet of sanity", as Mr. G. M. Trevelyan calls him), and yet works with such romantic exuberance and has such a delight in a darkly oracular manner that he appears the interpreter of some elaborate and esoteric cult.

Meredith's attitude to Nature can best be understood if it is compared with that of a greater poet, Wordsworth, who has, however, a slighter claim than Meredith to be considered *the* poet of Nature. To Wordsworth, Man was really a stranger in this world, with a heaven behind him, and unless he was constantly quickened by vision, reminded of infinity, he sank into the mere routine of sense; the shades of the prison-house closed upon him and he was a lost spirit. But Nature could become at certain moments the vesture of the eternal reality, the great mystery, whose light shone through, illumining the world with apocalyptic gleams. It is to the poet as the crystal is to the seer. Once some aspect of Nature becomes intensely real to Wordsworth it immediately loses that reality to become the window into the one enduring reality, into infinity. That is why he is the poet of solitude, for such moments only come in solitude, usually in lonely waste places and in scenes of natural grandeur. All his most characteristic and beautiful poems present to us a moment when

> The outward shows of sky and earth,
> Of hill and valley, . . .

suddenly become transfigured and the poet loses himself in an apocalyptic vision. It is significant that perhaps the most familiar phrase we have to describe this sense of the earthly suddenly becoming unearthly, to wit, "the light that never was on sea or land", should be his. Nearly all his poetry of Nature is an attempt to show that we can, in a measure, recapture at moments, through her agency, "the glory and the dream", whose passing he celebrates in his famous ode. He still sees man as an exile.

But to Meredith there are no lost Edens and burning remembrances of Heaven; Man is not exiled here for a term, but is himself a creature of Earth, a product, the highest we know, of Nature, who becomes conscious of herself in him. There are two well-known lines of Wordsworth's that, curiously enough, can be more aptly applied to Meredith's attitude than to their author's:

> Nature never did betray
> The heart that loved her, . . .

a deep-seated belief that finds its expression directly
or indirectly in so much of Meredith's work, whether
he is describing, in a lyric, a moment when he turns
to her in sorrow and desolation, or tells us how one
of his characters, like Diana of the Crossways, renews
her strength and confidence and sanity in the face of
Nature. And this is because we are Earth's creatures,
drawing our primary sustenance from Nature:

> On her great venture, Man,
> Earth gazes while her fingers dint the breast
> Which is his well of strength, his home of rest,
> And fair to scan. . . .

He is not merely a poet who has accepted Evolution,
he is essentially the poet *of* Evolution; not of a mere
mechanical progress or change but, at least when we
come to Man, of conscious striving. In this respect,
instead of escaping his age, he is its veritable singer.
Man is back again on the Earth. He is Nature's
experiment, her consciousness, her voice—

> Earth was not Earth, before her sons appeared;

and again—

> And order, high discourse,
> And decency, than which is life less dear,
> She has of him: the lyre of language clear,
> Love's tongue and source.

He does not accept this · fact reluctantly, because
he is compelled to do so, wistfully banishing angelic
dreams, and putting away, with a sigh, the tapestries
and furniture of Lost Paradises; he welcomes it and
makes it glow with wonder and poetry. Once these
heavenly lights, so cunningly adapted to our individual

gaze, are dimmed, Earth itself, the life stirring about us, begins to take on brighter hues and to glow and flame. Nature is no longer a dream that may turn at times into a vision, bodying forth the inner reality, but it is itself the only reality; it is our life. Meredith does not deny the existence of a central mystery, the why and wherefore of it all, the secret that is hidden away in the bosom of Earth, who drives us on and whose face we try to read:

> And ever that old task
> Of reading what he is and whence he came,
> Whither to go, finds wilder letters flame
> Across her mask; . . .

but he accepts the mystery and leaves the secret there, being at heart a poet and moralist and not seeking cosmological adventures.

So far as he did consider the universe at large he would probably subscribe to the old Kabbalistic axiom: "That which is above is in proportion with that which is below, and that which is below is in proportion with that which is above". We can reason confidently from that which we know to that which is unknown. If the Earth affords us no measure of satisfaction, it is unlikely that the universe will; for here we have grown, from the rose in the blood to the rose in the brain, and if this is not our home, then are we homeless indeed. When Meredith reaches out to the whole universe, as in his "Meditation under Stars", it is only to return to Earth with renewed wonder. He returns to see

> Her mists, her streaming gold,
> A wonder edges the familiar face:
> She wears no more that robe of printed hours;
> Half strange seems Earth, and sweeter than her flowers.

And not because she has become the mere vesture of
something outside herself, some reality shining through,
but because, breaking the dull spell of custom, he
sees Earth, the dust out of which all loveliness has
flowered, as she really is. But lovely or unlovely, kind
or cruel, Earth is all we have; even the very aspirations
that may lead us, if we are unwise, to deny her have
their roots in her strength and fullness; man expresses
her:

> And her desires are those.
> For happiness, for lastingness, for light.
> 'Tis she who kindles in his haunting night
> The hoped dawn-rose. . . .

Why then, Man and Earth, being so close, should
he ever have denied her? Why is not everything in
an exquisite harmony? The answer is that she has
produced in him a self-conscious being, and with
self-consciousness comes the Self. This is his glory
and this is his danger. It is his glory, for, through
thought and ever-increasing self-consciousness, he can
go forward expressing Earth as she wishes to be
expressed, if, that is, he will first consent to learn her
laws; he can be "Her lord, if to her rigid laws he
bows". It is his danger because the Self sometimes
takes command, bids him turn back and learn no more.
It conjures forth dream after pitiful dream, painting
the universe in the fashion of his indulgence, his every
childish desire, till the deluded human cannot see
aright the dust under his feet or the stars above his
head for the huge sprawling shadow that Self has
thrown upon the universe. He cannot live for fear
of dying. Meredith saw in religion, as it is usually
presented and understood, the shadow of this monstrous

Egoism, misshaping all life in its desire to proffer easy consolation, destroying the proper balance and paralysing rightful effort. It is through these cosy and painted chambers that he is for ever sending his east winds. For him there are no royal roads, no tricks of magic, to make all easy, and whatever would suggest that there are is only fostering illusion. His novels are filled with such shattered illusions and with selves emerging from them shivering and naked. His first story sounded the theme when it proclaimed an Ordeal. He sees men as mountaineers. But though there is the steep upward track, there is no summit within sight: "Spirit raves not for a goal"; our part is strife and effort, the "struggle to be wise", and while we strive we are gaining the best that life can offer, for this *is* living. Strength, he tells us, is gained only by service, trained by endurance, shaped by devotion: "Strength is not won by miracle or rape".

Though Meredith sets Man's feet firmly on the ground, this does not mean that Nature to him is wholly good. Like his contemporaries, he saw the reddened tooth and claw, and has, indeed, some very forceful and memorable passages, in his poetry, on this very subject, but he did not make the mistake, common then and since, of making a nightmare of her cruelty. We have a trick of looking down on the elaborate carnage of Nature, shudderingly noting her ghastly devices for maiming and rending her creatures, and at the same time unconsciously endowing such creatures with our own nerves and, in a praiseworthy attempt at imaginative sympathy, monstrously exaggerating their sufferings. It is as if a being as far above us as we are above the lower creatures should look down into our drawing-rooms and, noting there the passions and prejudices at work, should recoil in horror, having given us his own exquisite sensitiveness and forgetting for the moment that we are more coarsely fashioned. Meredith himself, in an interview, touched this point when he remarked: "We are all hunted more or less. Yet Nature is very kind to all her offspring. If you are a fine runner and your blood is up, you don't, in point of fact, feel a half of what you do when lying in bed or sitting in a chair thinking about it." But though it is a sound point, which should be brought to the notice of supersensitive persons kept awake by the thought of the sufferings of spiders or lobsters, men are for the most part still too insensitive for such a line of argument to do more good than harm. And Meredith's remarks above, made when he was an old man in a criticism of Tolstoy's doctrine, are a shade too complacent to be typical of his attitude. He saw the cruelty in Nature and was for ever insistent upon her drastic treatment. He believed that she is the source of our strength, and that she can be conquered by being obeyed, but that Man must not be her slave. There is always good in her, constantly welling up, but there is also evil, changing as we progress. There comes a point where what is "natural" has to be set aside, at the dictates of reason, and this point, as it were, travels forward as we ourselves move forward. But this does not lead us to the old war of spirit and sense, out of which have sprung so many of humanity's follies and illusions. That way lie asceticism and sensualism, both of which set aside reason and nature, and are indeed among those fantastic and unhealthy projections of the Ego which were Meredith's natural prey. To come closer to the relation between Man and Nature, as he understands it, we must first see what he makes of Man.

Meredith recognises the fact that at the root of Man's life are his animal instincts, and that it is his business not to efface them but to use them. The blood, giving him energy, the senses, through which he approaches this world and his fellows, these are not evil in themselves, are even good in themselves, but can be ill used. He sees that animal life is not something to be gradually eliminated, but the broad foundation of our spiritual life. We are not going up in a balloon, but building a tower.. The instincts determine, as it were, the pattern of our life which Nature has traced for us, and we mutilate this design at our peril. It is not our business to murder the bounding animal in us, dreaming insanely over his ebbing blood, but to tame him and ride him, rejoicing in his swiftness and strength. The body must be disciplined but not subdued, for brain and soul, its leaders and not its enemies, will have need of its vital energy. Without it they are lost. Meredith is one of the few modern writers who can talk of physical delights, the pleasures of the body, simply and naturally, without either that faintly apologetic or aggressive manner that hints so much. He seems to breathe Hellenic air and turns on the body the clear unshadowed eyes of the nobler pagans. No reader of his can fail to have remarked what exquisite play he makes with such a word as "blood", "sweet blood" as he so often calls it, when one of his heroines is before him, until a word whose common associations are rather unpleasant than not is able to fire whole trains of delightful

imagery in the mind. He turns blood into wine.
There is behind all this, of course, his own abounding
physical energy and gusto, the immense walker and
climber and juggler with huge iron bars. He does not
make the invalid's mistake of over-emphasising the
importance of mere physical strength and animal
exuberance, but he proclaims their value and expresses
their delights. At the same time, being in possession
of them himself (at least for the greater part of his life,
and certainly during the time when he formed his
opinions) and knowing exactly what they are worth, he
insists everywhere upon discipline. It is not, however, the mediæval discipline of asceticism, but the more
healthful and infinitely saner Greek discipline of
athletics. All his principal characters, certainly all the
men and most of the women, are athletes, whose feats
of pedestrianship are as carefully recorded as their
witticisms. And the discipline involved in these
athletics of his is the discipline of the nursery rather
than the discipline of the gaol, for there is behind it a
delighted recognition and love of the body and not
a lurking antagonism, compounded of a mingled fear
and contempt. He would send the blood humming
through its arteries, harden the thews and muscles,
clear the channels of the senses; and he would do all
this because Man is not his complete self unless his
body is fully alive. Brain and soul will be all the
healthier for this ruder health of their companion.
He has to achieve a harmony and the bass must be in
tune.

This harmony is one of three elements—blood,
brain, and spirit. A few lines from "The Woods of
Westermain" give us the whole matter:

Each of each in sequent birth,
Blood and brain and spirit, three
(Say the deepest gnomes of Earth)
Join for true felicity.
Are they parted, then expect
Some one sailing will be wrecked:
Separate hunting are they sped,
Scan the morsel coveted.
Earth that Triad is: she hides
Joy from him who that divides;
Showers it when the three are one,
Glassing her in union. . . .

Here we have the mutual dependence of the three
elements emphasised, the necessity for their harmonic
union stressed, and threats of what will happen if they
are discordant. It is, as we shall see, no little part of
Meredith's task as a novelist to show us how these
three are often parted and how "some one sailing"
is either wrecked or is speeded "between the ascetic
rocks and the sensual whirlpools" only at the last
gasping moment. It is not, however, very easy to
distinguish between "brain" and "spirit", and
Meredith is not consistent in his use of the terms.
Sometimes, indeed more often than not, "brain"
simply means the intellect, which, when in harmony
with the body, together with it brings forth spirit or
soul. Meredith sees the soul—in Mr. G. M.
Trevelyan's excellent phrase—as "the flushing of the
brain by the blood, of the cold intellectual by the hot
animal". The development of the intellect alone,
making Man into a logic-chopping machine or a
monster of will, has no attractions for Meredith (as it
has, for example, for Mr. Bernard Shaw, who has never
been able to free himself from the old ascetic trap), and
indeed such an inharmonious development, destroying
the sacred balance, is Meredith's natural prey.

Yet sometimes we discover him talking as if it was brain alone that mattered. "More brain, O Lord, more brain!" he cries in "Modern Love". "Never is earth misread by brain", he tells us in another place, and later looks forward to the time when "brain-rule splendidly towers". There seems to be some inconsistency here. The fact is that in these passages, and sometimes elsewhere, Meredith does not mean by "brain" what is commonly understood by "intellect"—the observing, classifying, analysing faculty, untouched by emotion—but the universal rationalising power that gives man true insight and enables him to bring harmony into his life. Coleridge, following Kant, made great play with a distinction between the Understanding and the Reason. It is this Reason of Coleridge's, this harmonising principle which is perhaps the secret of great genius, that Meredith frequently worships as "brain". So considered, "brain" ("irradiated thought", as Mr. Basil de Sélincourt happily names it) is hardly to be distinguished from "spirit" or "soul". Frequently as a process, it figures as "brain", and as a result, as something to be achieved, it figures as "spirit". But for the most part he sees Man as a balance of blood, brain, and spirit, and it is this harmony, as we shall see, he has in mind when he comes to examine men's lives in detail.

Meredith has been called an optimist. Actually his attitude eludes both optimism and pessimism; but if no escape is allowed, if the alternative is pressed, then he must be considered an optimist. His temperament was certainly optimistic, even if his creed was not, and his attitude is really a kind of stoicism coloured with the poet's native optimism, his fine ardent temper. Moreover, unlike so many of the greater literary figures of the latter half of the nineteenth century, he does definitely escape from pessimism. He does not believe in a malicious deity, a hostile universe in which Man, a naked shivering stranger, is nothing but a target for the heavy shafts of doom. Nor does he see him caught, a fluttering soul, in the monstrous machinery of matter, to be obliterated at the next tremor of a wheel. Meredith fights the pessimists as sturdily as he does the shallow optimists. Both of them make the mistake of not coming to terms with facts and of trying to impose a dream upon life. The shallow optimists, contriving for a season to shut out the world, succeed for a while in this imposition; the pessimists are those who have failed, who have suddenly awakened to find their dream gone, and who can be heard crying out in the darkness. But Meredith is far removed from either of them, and sees them still walking within the closed circle of the Self. That, indeed, is their error. We do not rightly begin to live until we begin to forget ourselves, looking outward, as it were, with all the eyes of our mind; and if, for our greater ease, we shut ourselves up, then life will come trampling in, sooner or later, withering away our fancies, scattering our card-castles, and we shall end in misery.

Freely accepting Evolution, Meredith takes up a position that Christian apologetics, in some quarters, has adopted since: he recognises that the Earth that has produced our needs is capable of satisfying them, that there is a good in her to match the good in us. But she only rewards those who understand her and serve her; there is no magical formula that will bring her bounty showering down upon us; in the last resort her desires are ours, and indeed are finding expression through the self-consciousness with which she has endowed us; but if we try to cut the cord that binds us, if we are too impatient or cowardly or purely self-seeking, then we do not serve her purposes and she punishes us. This is the lesson we have to learn, our ordeal. Meredith does not attempt to indicate ends and goals, nor does he ever grapple with ultimate values. His philosophy is, as it were, a stout staff for the ardent wayfarer and a rod of correction. It presupposes a keen zest for life and a belief in its fundamental goodness. This belief, which does not mean that all our dreams will come true, but only that Life will inevitably respond to the right demands, and that the right demands are, in the last resort, better than our idle dreams, Meredith calls Faith, and it plays a considerable part in his philosophy. It is Reason "tiptoe at the ultimate bound of her wit". But it is not a narcotic, only a little breathing-space between battle and battle, a moment's halt on the mountain-side, until Reason is ready to go forward again. Meredith believes that living, to be worthy of the name, is striving.

We have called this philosophy a stout staff for the ardent wayfarer, for persons of an eager radical reforming temper, and a rod of correction for the egoists, the sensualists, the ascetics, whimpering by the roadside. To admit it is all this is to say a great deal in its favour, but the metaphor suggests certain limitations. It is a philosophy for persons who already have their values and are not asking to be roused from despair. Meredith, like many men of strong individuality who have had trouble with their Egos, was pleased to accept a system in which the individual could hardly find a place, and was really impatient with people who were wistful of such things as personal survival. When he cries—

> Into the breast that gives the rose
> Shall I with shuddering fall?

we applaud his brave gesture, but we do not feel that, for example, Claudio, crying, "Ay, but to die, and go we know not where", has been answered. It is this cry and not the complacent question of the pantheist that lingers longest in our ears. There is perhaps nothing better in this life than a courageous acceptance of death, as Meredith himself has observed, but this means a steadfast disregard of very natural fear; persons who tell us, as Meredith sometimes did, that death is merely going from one room to another are rightly suspect; we feel that the philosopher is so occupied rounding off his system that he has not yet squarely faced the fact of death, his imagination chancing to be otherwise engaged. Pantheism is actually neither a religion nor a philosophy, but a certain poetical state of mind, which leads us to see everything so touched with wonder and beauty that we call it God; but it is inevitable that after a time we are compelled to realise that if everything is God, nothing is God. We have merely borrowed a deeply significant word, and gradually some parts of reality will appear more God-like than others, until we wake to discover our pantheism gone.

The so-called pantheism of Meredith was only this occasional poetical state of mind, an uprush of elemental wonder. For the rest, he can talk of gods, by which he means the laws of our being and of Nature, which is probably all that gods ever were. He can also, on occasion, talk of God, who is, to him as to many of his contemporaries, the somewhat bleak personification of a kind of ethical progress. He can even remark on the value of prayer and commend it as a practice, but it must be prayer without a direct object, and as it is obviously also an appeal without a hearer, it is clearly nothing to him but a psychological safety-valve. That prayer is an excellent psychological safety-valve, an act to be commended by any physician of the mind, is certainly true, but it is equally certain that any one who sees the act of prayer in this light, and only in this light, is for ever debarred from it. You cannot cultivate simple faith, nor decide, after elaborate introspection and reasoning, to act upon impulse. This little point on the subject of Meredith's attitude towards prayer is worth making, not because it is of any great importance in his scheme of things, but because it is a good example of a certain weakness in his general philosophic attitude. This weakness cannot, with any justice, be called downright insincerity, but it is a kind of oracular complacency that leaves one with a suspicion that the philosopher has not only refrained from testing the logical consistency of his conclusions—and that we hardly expect from a poet and novelist—but, what is far graver, he has not compared them with his real experience, the actual stuff of life. His attitude towards death, already noticed, is an excellent example of this weakness. We feel that he is deliberately shutting off his imagination from the fact in order to maintain a certain attitude. On one occasion, in talk, Meredith ridiculed the time-old melancholy of autumn and pointed out that we do not feel sad when we change our coats. Here, again, we cannot help feeling that either the speaker was insensitive (and we know that he was not) or that he was deliberately making light of a universal and very profound state of mind for purposes of his own. You cannot blot out regret at the passing of beauty, the coming of darkness, the withering of the world, the decay and death of *these* flowers, *these* leaves, with a reference to the changing of coats. It is, of course, possible that you have succeeded so well in escaping from human frailties and in merging yourself in the universal mind, which may possibly see in this season only a change of coats, that you can take up this attitude in all sincerity, but it is also possible that you are merely pretending, saying "Not at home" to inconvenient but by no means dishonourable emotions, just as Sir Willoughby Patterne said "Not at home" to the lieutenant of Marines; which means that you are, for the moment, not more than a man but somewhat less than one. It is a tribute to any system to say that it will not admit such things as regret and melancholy, if only the philosopher has dealt honestly with them and with his own and our experience. Meredith will not admit such feelings, but, in doing so, he maintains a certain determined brightness, a glitter, that arouses suspicion. There are moments when the fragrant drift of smoke, through which we have caught so many memorable utterances, thins away from the face of the oracle and we catch sight of nothing but a gilded mask, whose moving lips frame for us resounding but idle words.

But this weakness must not blind us to the real force

and splendour of Meredith's attitude. Sometimes
there may be nothing but the gilded mask, but more
often than not there is that sensitive and ardent face,
glowing with real thought and emotion. He has his
own defects, as we have seen, but he is free from all the
characteristic weaknesses of the age in which he lived,
the age from which he contrived to escape. That
sense of strain, which we have remarked in so many of
his contemporaries, is replaced in him by a splendid
buoyancy and completeness. He is untouched, too, by
that curious suggestion of intellectual vulgarity or even
squalor that taints so many of the Victorian thinkers.
And by throwing the emphasis away from either a
cast-iron mechanical universe or a harassed and bewildered human soul, one or other of which occupied so
many of his fellows to the exclusion of everything else,
by achieving so early a synthesis, bridging the Nature-
Man gulf, and not only accepting evolution but building on it from the first—by doing all this, he was
able to touch two extremes, supported at all points
by his philosophy, that were not touched by any other
single writer of the century. He was able to see Man
against the background of Nature, and to see Man
against the background of a very complex social life.
He could rhapsodise over a skylark as well as Wordsworth could, and yet could pounce upon an absurd
remark as quickly as Jane Austen. He could be as
observant and as contented in the fields as Richard
Jefferies, and yet be as subtle in the drawing-room as
Henry James. As a poet, he comes perhaps closer to
Nature, not only in his talk *about* her but in his actual
appreciation of her sights and sounds, his feeling for
her moods, than any other poet in our literature. As

a novelist, he handles the significant minutiæ of intercourse in a highly sophisticated and complex social life
perhaps more exquisitely than any other English writer.
As a philosopher, he was able to link up both these
unusual capacities, to join together the wildest woods
and the wittiest dinner-table, to take us through the
darkest thickets of introspection and subtle analysis
and yet keep the south-west wind still blowing about
our ears and the sunshine still pouring down upon our
heads.

CHAPTER IV

During the greater part of his life, Meredith's verse, as we have seen, was not appreciated nor even widely read. He began and ended his literary career with poetry and preferred to be thought a poet, but it was his fiction that made him famous. Yet by some curious chance his poetry has been the subject of more intelligent criticism than his prose, and at least half-a-dozen critics of repute have given us studies of the verse. Its definitely gnomic and didactic character, however, has encouraged such critics to deal at length with Meredith the thinker rather than with Meredith the literary artist, and their studies spend more time with the attitude of mind of which the verse is the expression than with the actual verse itself. In this place, having already devoted considerable space to this attitude of mind, we are now at liberty to examine his verse rather more closely. It may turn out to be a profitable venture; it will certainly be a hazardous one. Meredith is one of our most difficult poets, not merely because he is tough and frequently obscure, but because any estimate of his work raises questions that cannot be properly answered without some reference to the scope and nature of Poetry itself, so that the critic

86

is faced with the alternative of either making what
may appear sweeping and unsupported statements or
writing yet another *Poetics,* in which Meredith and all
his works would be lost and finally buried. And there
can be no question as to which alternative must be
preferred here, where there are plainly no facilities for
any excursions into æsthetics.

A further proof of this difficulty, if one should be
needed, is furnished by the extraordinarily diverse
judgements that have been passed, and are still being
passed, upon his poetry. He is everything from
Apollo to a corncrake. Sober and by no means insensitive persons open the Poetical Works at random,
confront us with some such passage as—

> But with rhetoric loose, can we check man's brute?
> Assemblies of men on their legs invoke
> Excitement for wholesome diversion: there shoot
> Electrical sparks between their dry thatch
> And thy waved torch, more to kindle than light.
> 'Tis instant between you: the trick of a catch
>   (To match a Batrachian croak)
> Will thump them a frenzy or fun in their veins.
> Then may it be rather the well-worn joke
> Thou repeatest, to stop conflagration, and write
> Penance for rhetoric. Strange will it seem,
> When thou readest that form of thy homage to brains!

and then trail a sardonic finger down the page to the
very climax of the poem ("The Empty Purse"), which
runs—

> And ask of thyself: This furious Yea
>   Of a speech I thump to repeat,
>   In the cause I would have prevail,
>   For seed of a nourishing wheat,
>   *Is it accepted of Song?*
>   Does it sound to the mind through the ear,
> Right sober, pure sane? has it disciplined feet?

It all seems as accepted of Song as a dish of hay is

accepted of dinner. There is meaning in the lines for one who will worry it out, just as there is sustenance in the hay for those able to digest it, but the one bears as much relation to poetry as the other does to food. Yet no sooner is Meredith brayed out of court, in this fashion, than he is brought in again and loaded with honours by critics of the highest repute. They ask us to remark his astonishing range, from the lilting May morning of "Love in the Valley" to the weighty *Odes in Contribution to the Song of French History,* from the subtle and tortured "Modern Love" to the shining Hellenic "Day of the Daughter of Hades". They proceed to analyse the poetry and disengage a number of undeniably great qualities, calling our attention to the weighty mass of original thought in it, the wit, the rich, flashing imagery, the metrical experiments, and so on and so forth, until we wonder if we are not faced with a great poetical genius. And, oddly enough, both parties are in the right, for those who taste and shudder are not without reason, and yet all the good qualities, discovered by the critics' analyses, are undoubtedly present in the work.

They are both right simply because this poetry of Meredith's, regarded as a whole, has a most curious character, making it so difficult to estimate. It might be compared to a very rich pudding, containing the most varied and delightful ingredients, that does not make friends with the palate because it has not been properly mixed and cooked. Meredith is a great man of letters who displays on occasion practically every quality necessary for a great poet but who only rarely turns himself into anything resembling a great poet. His range is extraordinary. Remembering such things as "The Empty Purse", "A Faith on Trial", "The Cageing of Ares", "The Sage Enamoured", and the various "Odes", we may say at once that he is harsh, crabbed, and tuneless, but immediately line after line rises from the memory to mock the judgement. We remember—

> When her mother tends her before the laughing mirror,
>   Tying up her laces, looping up her hair,
> Often she thinks, were this wild thing wedded,
>   More love should I have, and much less care, . . .

and all its lilting companion verses in a poem ("Love in the Valley") that has lost its appeal in some quarters only because it is considered too cloying. We remember such openings as—

> Sweet as Eden is the air,
>   And Eden-sweet the ray,

and

> O briar-scents, on yon wet wing
> Of warm South-west wind brushing by,
> You mind me of the sweetest thing
> That ever mingled frank and shy.

In one of the very poems mentioned above ("A Faith on Trial") we suddenly light on the lines beginning—

> I bowed as a leaf in rain;
> As a tree when the leaf is shed
> To winds in the season at wane. . . .

And even at the very last, in his old age, when his thought seems to be expressed in the very gravel and ashes of poetry, he can suddenly give us—

> They have no song, the sedges dry.
>   And still they sing.
> It is within my breast they sing,
>   As I pass by. . . .

And if we then imagine that he can show us nothing between the two extremes of the tuneless patter of so

many of his longer poems and this easy lyrical sweetness, memory or a fresh reading further confounds us.
He can touch the grand manner. His "Odes", in which
swift and tangled metaphor so often merely raises so
much dust, can open swingingly with—

> Days, when the ball of our vision
> Had eagles that flew unabashed to sun;
> When the grasp on the bow was decision,
> And arrow and hand and eye were one, . . .

or can come crashing out, in "Napoleon", with—

> Cannon his name,
> Cannon his voice, he came.
> Who heard of him, heard shaken hills,
> An earth at quake, to quiet stamped;
> Who looked on him beheld the will of wills,
> The driver of wild flocks where lions ramped. . . .

He can rise to a Miltonic height of mingled stress and
sweetness, as in those familiar lines—

> I say but that this love of Earth reveals
> A soul beside our own to quicken, quell,
> Irradiate, and through ruinous floods uplift;

or in the whole of that almost faultless little poem, "A
Ballad of Past Meridian", whose final verse runs—

> Life said, As thou hast carved me, such am I.
> Then memory, like the nightjar on the pine,
> And sightless hope, a woodlark in night sky,
> Joined notes of Death and Life till night's decline:
> Of Death, of Life, those inwound notes are mine.

Within the compass of one volume, his second, he
can move from the lilting garrulities of "Juggling
Jerry"—

> Pitch here the tent, while the old horse grazes:
>   By the old hedge-side we'll halt a stage.
> It's nigh my last above the daisies:
>   My next leaf'll be man's blank page, . . .

or "The Old Chartist"—

> But if I go and say to my old hen:
> I'll mend the gentry's boots, and keep discreet,
> Until they grow *too* violent,—why, then,
> A warmer welcome I might chance to meet. . . .

from these things to the sharply etched picture in the
"Ode to the Spirit of Earth in Autumn", in which we
are shown the stormy south-west wind descending upon
the autumn woods—

> . . . then sharp the woodland bore
> A shudder and a noise of hands:
> A thousand horns from some far vale
> In ambush sounding on the gale.
> Forth from the cloven sky came bands
> Of revel-gathering spirits; trooping down,
> Some rode the tree-tops; some on torn cloud-strips
> Burst screaming thro' the lighted town:
> And scudding seaward, some fell on big ships:
> Or mounting the sea-horses blew
> Bright foam-flakes on the black review
> Of heaving hulls and burying beaks. . . .

And thence to the more sublime conception and
imagery of "Lucifer in Starlight" (the very title, with
its suggestion of a great black bulk against the powdered
glitter of stars, creates a powerful and enduring image),
which, in spite of an occasional awkwardness, is one of
the greatest sonnets of the nineteenth century:

> On a starred night Prince Lucifer uprose.
> Tired of his dark dominion swung the fiend
> Above the rolling ball in cloud part screened,
> Where sinners hugged their spectre of repose.
> Poor prey to his hot fit of pride were those.
> And now upon his western wing he leaned,
> Now his huge bulk o'er Afric's sands careened,
> Now the black planet shadowed Arctic snows.
> Soaring through wider zones that pricked his scars
> With memory of the old revolt from Awe,
> He reached a middle height, and at the stars,

> Which are the brain of heaven, he looked, and sank.
> Around the ancient track marched, rank on rank,
> The army of unalterable law.

But in the same volume there is one single poem (or, if you will, a sequence of short poems on one theme) that shows, perhaps better than anything else, its creator's extraordinary range, and from which may be extracted examples of almost every kind of poetry. That poem, of course, is "Modern Love", in which, as Mr. Trevelyan has remarked, "Psychology, comedy, tragedy, irony, philosophy, and beauty follow upon each other's heels in such quick succession, that scarcely, except by a certain greater master, has a single tune been played upon so many stops". This is true, not only of the matter to be expressed, but also of the expression itself. Within his sixteen-line "mock sonnets" Meredith contrives to give us almost every kind of poetry. He rises from the purely epigrammatic, a witty thought neatly turned—

> How many a thing which we cast to the ground,
> When others pick it up becomes a gem!
> We grasp at all the wealth it is to them;
> And by reflected light its worth is found, . . .

to the heightened epigrammatic—

> Cold as a mountain in its star-pitched tent,
> Stood high Philosophy, less friend than foe:
> Whom self-caged Passion, from its prison-bars,
> Is always watching with a wondering hate.
> Not till the fire is dying in the grate,
> Look we for any kinship with the stars, . . .

and then on to passages in which emotion spurs the wit—

> A kiss is but a kiss now! and no wave
> Of a great flood that whirls me to the sea.
> But, as you will! we'll sit contentedly,
> And eat our pot of honey on the grave. . . .

The wit remains, concentrated and bitter, but it is taken up by a voice that sings, as in such lines as—

> My tears are on thee, that have rarely dropped
> As balm for any bitter wound of mine:
> My breast will open for thee at a sign!
> But, no: we are two reed-pipes, coarsely stopped:
> The God once filled them with his mellow breath;
> And they were music till he flung them down,
> Used! used! Hear now the discord-loving clown
> Puff his gross spirit in them, worse than death!

He will make pictures and create a great romantic phrase in the old fashion of poetry—

> In our old shipwrecked days there was an hour,
> When in the firelight steadily aglow,   .
> Joined slackly, we beheld the red chasm grow
> Among the clicking coals. Our library-bower
> That eve was left to us: and hushed we sat
> As lovers to whom Time is whispering, . . .

and he will bring together words that create very vivid images and at the same time suggest, by their very sound, the emotion of the onlooker—

> Mark where the pressing wind shoots javelin-like
> Its skeleton shadow on the broad-backed wave!
> Here is a fitting spot to dig Love's grave;
> Here where the ponderous breakers plunge and strike,
> And dart their hissing tongues high up the sand. . . .

He can give us a whole stanza of melodious fullness and romantic beauty like that verse xlvii. which was Swinburne's favourite:

> We saw the swallows gathering in the sky,
> And in the osier-isle we heard them noise.
> We had not to look back on summer joys,
> Or forward to a summer of bright dye:
> But in the largeness of the evening earth
> Our spirits grew as we went side by side.
> The hour became her husband and my bride.
> Love, that had robbed us so, thus blessed our dearth!

The pilgrims of the year waxed very loud
In multitudinous chatterings, as the flood
Full brown came from the West, and like pale blood
Expanded to the upper crimson cloud.
Love, that had robbed us of immortal things,
This little moment mercifully gave,
Where I have seen across the twilight wave
The swan sail with her young beneath her wings.

The range of the man who wrote this one poem is clearly beyond that of all but the three or four greatest poets in our literature, and, as we have seen, it by no means exhausts Meredith's command of the poetical instrument. Of his literary genius, and the breadth and fullness of that genius, there can be no question.

He had genius, all the fertility of imagination and un-resting vigour of intellect claimed for him by his most enthusiastic critics; but his genius is not altogether poetical genius. He is undoubtedly a poet, a considerable poet, but he is not a great poet. The qualities in which he is deficient may seem trifling when compared with the sum of his powers, but unfortunately they happen to be the very qualities that make the poet and distinguish him from other men of literary genius, from the novelist, the essayist, the critic, the philosopher. It is true that his prose, with its disdain of logical development and its incredibly swift movement from metaphor to metaphor, seems very close to poetry. When we read his novels we are constantly reminded of the poet. But then when we turn to the poetry we find ourselves back again in the company of the novelist and philosopher. He seems to be master of a medium that is somewhere between poetry and prose, but the man who uses it is more successful when he is considered as a prose writer and not as a poet. It may be said that such criticism has always been directed against work that is highly original, as Mr. Trevelyan seems to hint when he says: ". . . We have a hundred kinds of poetry. Of these kinds Mr. Meredith has created one. . . ." Other men of original genius in verse have been told that they were clever dogs but no poets, and Time has inevitably clapped such pieces of criticism into its pillory. There is, for example, Browning. But actually there is very little force in the objection. Browning and Meredith, as Wilde's famous epigram reminds us, have much in common. They both began with work of a kind we least associate with their names, decorative and mellifluous verses that suggest that their authors had newly risen from a study of Keats. They both developed, as time went on, a highly original and personal manner of their own, which was, in both instances, somewhat obscure, crabbed, and harsh. But there is one difference between them. Faced with some things that Browning wrote, we may possibly wish that he had never written them at all; we may dislike them intensely as poetry; but nevertheless we cannot imagine them as anything else but poetry. He may turn himself at times into the very Caliban of poetry, but he remains a poet. Queer as the result of it may be, the impulse, we may say, is always a poetical one.

With Meredith, the impulse is not always a poetical one. Let it be understood at once that criticism of this kind must be based on the work itself. It is nothing to us what a writer felt so long as his work makes *us* feel something. A writer's attitude of mind is not the criterion of his work. But if we find there is something wrong with the work, as we do with so much that Meredith wrote, then we are justified in trying to account for the deficiency in the attitude of the writer himself. Meredith was a poet only on very rare occasions. A great deal of his verse fails, making us feel that we should have preferred the substance of it to have been embodied in some prose form, because the writer, for all his great gifts, is not feeling as a poet should feel. In the first place, his attitude is too frequently coldly didactic, and his words are not sufficiently charged with emotion. A comparison with other poets will make this clearer. Meredith's long poem "A Faith on Trial" is at once deeply personal and philosophical; it describes how the poet, still half-stunned by a recent bereavement, goes walking in the countryside that reminds him poignantly of his loss, looks at the Earth he has loved so well, and ends by reasserting certain beliefs that have been challenged by the blow that has fallen upon him. It would be difficult to single out a poem that must have meant more to the poet himself, for it expresses a very significant mood, an awful moment in his life, and it is, at the same time, one of the longest expositions of his creed. Therefore, to compare one of its most important and best-known passages with certain lines from Wordsworth's *Tintern Abbey* and Coleridge's *Dejection* is not unfair to Meredith.

Here is the passage from "A Faith on Trial":

> 'They see not above or below;
> 'Farthest are they from my soul,'
> Earth whispers: 'they scarce have the thirst,
> 'Except to unriddle a rune;
> 'And I spin none; only show,
> 'Would humanity soar from its worst,
> 'Winged above darkness and dole,
> 'How flesh unto spirit must grow.
> 'Spirit raves not for a goal.

'Shapes in man's likeness hewn
'Desires not; neither desires
'The sleep or the glory: it trusts;
'Using my gifts, yet aspires;
'Dreams of a higher than it.
'The dream is an atmosphere;
'A scale still ascending to knit
'The clear to the loftier Clear.
' 'Tis Reason herself, tiptoe
'At the ultimate bound of her wit,
'On the verges of Night and Day . . .

Compare this with Wordsworth's

       . . For I have learned
To look on nature, not as in the hour
Of thoughtless youth; but hearing oftentimes
The still, sad music of humanity,
Nor harsh nor grating, though of ample power
To chasten and subdue. And I have felt
A presence that disturbs me with the joy
Of elevated thoughts; a sense sublime
Of something far more deeply interfused,
Whose dwelling is the light of setting suns,
And the round ocean and the living air,
And the blue sky, and in the mind of man;
A motion and a spirit, that impels
All thinking things, all objects of all thought,
And rolls through all things. . . .

And again with Coleridge's

O Lady! we receive but what we give,
And in our life alone does Nature live:
Ours is her wedding-garment, ours her shroud!
  And would we ought behold, of higher worth,
Than that inanimate cold world allowed
To the poor loveless ever-anxious crowd,
  Ah! from the soul itself must issue forth
A light, a glory, a fair luminous cloud
    Enveloping the Earth—
And from the soul itself must there be sent
  A sweet and potent voice, of its own birth,
Of all sweet sounds the life and element!

Now, as thought, something that can be paraphrased
into prose, the Meredith passage is as satisfactory as

the other two: indeed it may be said to be more comprehensive and rise higher than either of the others. But as poetry, with which we are now concerned, it is clearly far less satisfying. In spite of its swiftness, it has a prose air. The marriage of thought and song has not been consummated. Meredith seems to us an excited talker rather than a moved and moving singer; the thought calls for sublimity, a large symphonic movement, but instead of this, it is given a thin snip-snap, a brittle aphoristic manner. It provides us with a number of memorable aphorisms (which are themselves the reason why so many philosophically-minded persons, not over-fond of poetry, have been enthusiastic about Meredith), but the lines have not that haunting quality peculiar to poetry. Mr. Trevelyan has singled out the haunting quality of so much of Meredith's verse as one of its most pronounced characteristics, but he seems to be in danger of confusing what are simply memorable aphorisms and epigrams (such as "Slave is the open mouth beneath the closed", and "We drank the pure daylight of honest speech"), in which a thought is crystallised in a brisk phrase, with something very different, those great passages or lines in which poetry becomes sheer magic, those miraculous fusions of thought, imagery, and sound, that are really haunting. Again, though the Meredith passage contains any number of metaphors, indeed there is a new one in almost every line, for the poet is following his usual practice of leaping swiftly from one to the other, yet these metaphors hardly rise to the dignity of imagery, and they leave the imagination starved; whereas the Wordsworth and Coleridge passages, rich as they are in

imagery whose resources are, as it were, allowed to be
fully explored by the reader's imagination, come to the
mind with a satisfying fullness. The result of all this
is that the two older poets appear to be making a full
communication of the kind necessary to poetry, while
the other is only making a partial communication.
One seems to come from both the heart and the mind,
the other only from the mind. Meredith, seeming
to ask for little more than intellectual acquiescence, is
commenting on life: Wordsworth and Coleridge,
whose thought is borne forward on a tide of emotion,
are expressing life.

Milton once said that poetry "is simple, sensuous,
passionate", a definition that was applauded, on more
than one occasion, by Coleridge. It does not tell us
all about poetry, but it does lay a finger on three
characteristics that are essential; the absence of even
one of them is perilous. A great deal of Meredith's
verse, while it has all manner of good qualities, is
neither simple, nor sensuous, nor passionate. That is
what we mean when we say that the mind of Meredith,
though undoubtedly the mind of a man of literary
genius, is only infrequently the mind of a poet, which
should be itself simple (that is, in Coleridge's words,
without "affectation and morbid peculiarity"), sensuous, and passionate. He lacks that instinctive sense
of form which makes the poet. The results of this
deficiency can be seen in many different directions in
his work. There is first that obscurity which has
taken up so much of his critics' time. At its worst it
cannot be defended, but for much of what the ordinary
reader finds both ugly to read and difficult to comprehend, certain pleas have been made by friendly critics.

They point out that Meredith's mind works like lightning, that—in the words of one of them—"He weeds out the commonplace and the unessential", passing rapidly from metaphor to metaphor, and so makes an unusually severe demand on the reader's attention. All this is perfectly true; it is the inevitable inference from it, namely, that once you have puzzled out the meaning of the lines they become poetry; that is not true, as we shall see. Another line of defence, rarely put forward but actually of greater force than the other, is that Meredith, by the nature of his thought and beliefs, with which his poetry has to do, cannot help being obscure. He is not in a tradition; he has no ready-made symbols, but must, like Blake (whose obscurity partly proceeds from the same cause), manufacture his own, and unless these are understood the meaning cannot be caught. The reader, therefore, has to do two things instead of one: he has not only to comprehend the meaning of the poet's words in combination, he has also to puzzle out the special meaning of some of the individual words, otherwise the whole passage is nonsense. This can be illustrated very simply by a glance at one of Meredith's most charming short lyrics, "Wind on the Lyre":

> That was the chirp of Ariel
> You heard as overhead it flew,
> The farther going more to dwell,
> And wing our green to wed our blue. . . .

In the last line, unless you grasp the significance of the two symbols "green" and "blue", which represent Earth and Heaven, the meaning is lost. This difficulty of a special symbolism, inevitable in a mystical or philosophical poet who stands outside a tradition,

runs throughout Meredith's verse, and many of his
more important poems, such things as the sublimely
conceived "Hymn to Colour", cannot be appreciated
until his own ready-made symbolism is grasped.

But his obscurity, of course, can hardly be excused
on these grounds. We must now return to the first
line of defence, which points out Meredith's swift
movement and compression and avoidance of the
merely commonplace, and tells us that a little extra
attention on the part of the reader will make all well.
A poet who is "difficult" in this way is in a strong
position with many readers, because they feel that
their appreciation immediately raises them above the
common herd. If you confess that you find much of
this verse tough and unpalatable, you are in danger
of being set down as an indolent trifler. Meredith
enthusiasts have not scrupled to use this weapon.
But they themselves, it would seem, are apt to mistake
the thrill of triumph of the puzzle-solver for the
genuine æsthetic thrill. The point to be considered
is whether a delighted discovery of the meaning turns
this tough matter into poetry. Great passages of
verse, it is true, have a habit of taking on an increasing
value and significance with familiarity, but this must
not be confused with Meredithian fog and daylight.
When we first encounter such a poem as "Earth's Pre-
ference" (a comparatively simple example) and read—

> Earth loves her young: a preference manifest:
> She prompts them to her fruits and flower-beds;
> Their beauty with her choicest interthreads,
> And makes her revel of their merry zest;
> As in our East much were it in our West,
> If men had risen to do the work of heads.
> Her gabbling grey she eyes askant, nor treads
> The ways they walk; by what they speak oppressed.

How wrought they in their zenith? 'Tis not writ;
Not all; yet she by one sure sign can read:
Have they but held her laws and nature dear,
They mouth no sentence of inverted wit.
More prizes she her beasts than this high breed
Wry in the shape she wastes her milk to rear.

in which the mention of "inverted wit" seems almost
impudent, we feel that either the poet is rambling or
raving, or that he is being too subtle for us. But a
closer study reveals the fact that the theme is a comparatively simple one and that the poet is merely
restating some of his favourite ideas. Nature herself
prefers the young to the old, and the cynical wisdom
of the latter is simply a sign that they have misused
their own youth, have never come to terms with
Nature, and are outside her favour, worse than the
beasts. But having grasped the meaning, if necessary
phrase by phrase, we do not find the poetic value of the
lines any greater than they were before. The poem
retains its ugliness and awkwardness. Nor can we
help thinking, with this as with dozens of other things
that Meredith wrote, that had the poet felt more, he
would inevitably have been simpler in statement. We
cannot avoid the suspicion that he is idly twisting
phrases, that what we read is the result of an unusual
literary energy undirected by any emotion, merely
scrawling arabesques.

This crabbed uncouthness, this almost perverse
ugliness, is found in all Meredith's later poems. If
we free him from any suspicion of insincerity, that is,
from any charge of covering up matter of no great
moment with a false appearance of wit and profundity
(and we cannot do so entirely), we must set it down
to his lack of any instinctive sense of form. It is not

true to say that he had no ear. If he deliberately set himself to make an appeal to the ear (as in "Love in the Valley" and "Phoebus with Admetus", with their cunningly placed long stresses, and in "The Lark Ascending" and some other things), he showed great skill. But he has to be definitely experimenting, and when he is not, he does not appear to have an ear at all. Many of his longer poems are either in jerky gasps or in a tuneless patter, giving us neither rhythm nor cadence. Now and again, the music will break in, when he suddenly begins to feel something. It is impossible for any man of literary genius to feel strongly and not write to haunt the ear, and Meredith is no exception to the rule. But throughout much of his verse, he is not feeling anything; his attitude of mind is purely didactic and untouched by emotion; and not being an instinctive artist in this form, his ear never comes into play. Not a little of the so-called obscurity of his verse is simply the result of its ugly tunelessness; the eye travels down the page, but the ear refuses to listen, so that passage after passage is read, in the way that ordinary prose is read, but is not fully grasped. Nor if we stop, and wrestle with each line, making sure of the meaning, do we mend the matter, for such quarrying carries us still further away from poetic pleasure. We read poems of his that are packed with original ideas, brimmed with hard thinking, and yet what our memory carries away are those lines in which a sudden touch of emotion stops the shower of aphorisms and brings with it a cry, as when in "A Ballad of Fair Ladies in Revolt" the poet drops the brittle-pointed dialogue and cries—

Have women nursed some dream since Helen sailed,
Over the sea of blood the blushing star, . . .

or when after some rather shapeless and frigid musings on the Universe, in "Meditation under Stars", he returns to look at this world and his concluding lines blossom into loveliness:

> Then at new flood of customary morn,
>   Look at her through her showers,
>   Her mists, her streaming gold,
> A wonder edges the familiar face:
> She wears no more that robe of printed hours;
> Half strange seems Earth, and sweeter than her flowers.

Remembering then this lack of instinctive security in form, this uncertainty of touch, we should not be surprised to discover that he is often weakest when he would be most simple and direct. There are times, as we have seen already, when he achieves a direct lyrical simplicity. He does it admirably, for example, in his "Dirge in Woods":

> A wind sways the pines,
>   And below
> Not a breath of wild air;
> Still as the mosses that glow
> On the flooring and over the lines
> Of the roots here and there.
> The pine-tree drops its dead;
> They are quiet, as under the sea.
> Overhead, overhead
> Rushes life in a race,
> As the clouds the clouds chase;
>   And we go,
> And we drop like the fruits of the tree,
>   Even we,
>   Even so.

But for one triumph of this kind, there are dozens of failures, verses like—

> Her lamp he sees, and young desire
>   Is fed while cloaked she flies,
> She quivers shot of violet fire
>   To ash at look of eyes, . . .

or the last stanza of his "Mother to Babe":

> Life in light you glass
> When you peep and coo,
>   You, my little one, mine!
> Brooklet chirps to grass,
> Daisy looks in dew
>   Up to dear sunshine.

It may be said that these demonstrably bad verses are, after all, only the little failures by the way that could be matched in the collected works of almost any poet. But actually Meredith can partly ruin his major poems by thrusting upon them what can only be called downright bad craftsmanship. The verses of "Phoebus with Admetus" contain some of his richest poetry, a magnificent feast of imagery—

> Many swarms of wild bees descended on our fields:
>   Stately stood the wheatstalk with head bent high:
> Big of heart we laboured at storing mighty yields,
>   Wool and corn, and clusters to make men cry!

and even better—

> You with shelly horns, rams! and promontory goats,
>   You whose browsing beards dip in coldest dew!
> Bulls, that walk the pastures in kingly-flashing coats!

Yet to these verses he can attach a refrain, repeating it eight times, that is too involved to be the rustic chorus it pretends to be and too awkward to be anything else, an exasperating performance:

> God! of whom music
> And song and blood are pure,
> The day is never darkened
> That had thee here obscure.

The person responsible for this refrain can hardly have been on good terms with the deity he celebrates. Another poem almost ruined by the reiteration of two unlovely lines is "Earth and a Wedded Woman", of which the central idea, the suggested kinship between a lonely wife and the parched earth, is rather beautiful. But we come perilously near bathos when the poet insists on repeating, with some minor variations, at the conclusion of each verse:

> Rain! O the glad refresher of the grain!
> And welcome waterspouts, had we sweet rain!

It is this inability to deal beautifully with simple statements that makes the great mass of Meredith's ballads and pure narrative verse, in spite of occasionally great dramatic force, as in "The Nuptials of Attila", the weakest section of his poetical work, and one that, taken by itself, would give a reader a very false idea of the poet's real power.

There is yet one other important characteristic of Meredith's mind that must be examined. It is a subject that demands far more space than it can be given here, but it must be dealt with if only because the strength and weakness of his style, in both poetry and prose, cannot be understood without some reference to it. Meredith was both a poet and a thinker. He had at once an unusually fine and vigorous intellect and a rich and teeming imagination. His mind worked with lightning-like rapidity, one thought swiftly following upon the heels of another, and, being a poet, these thoughts of his set fire to a train of images. But the curious balance of intellect and imagination in him makes him use his imagery in a very peculiar way. Had he been more of a philosopher and less of a poet, he would have distrusted figurative language and taken refuge in abstractions. Had he been more of a poet and less of a thinker and a wit, he would have dallied longer with his images, exploring, as it were, their

sensuous beauty. But as it is, his imagination pours
out images while his thought presses forward, and we
see him leaping from metaphor to metaphor like a
man jumping from log to log across a river. And it
is essential that the reader should jump with him, or
should merely catch the flash of an image and then
pass forward to the next. As Mr. Trevelyan remarks:
"He drops each figure the moment that it has served
his purpose. He extracts from it one analogy, the
essential idea; then he is off to a new metaphor before
the old one has lost its bloom from too much handling.
. . . The picture must be seen, the idea read, in an
intellectual flash of lightning." This is his habit both
in prose and verse, though it is more marked, of course,
in the verse. Thus we open the "Poetical Works" at
random, and light upon such lines as these:

> Thou wilt not have our paths befouled
> By simulation; are we vile to view,
> The heavens shall see us clean of our own dust,
> Beneath thy breezy flitting wing:
> They make their mirror upon faces true;
> And where they win reflection, lucid heave
> The under tides of this hot heart seen through.
> Beneficently wilt thou clip
> All oversteppings of the plumed,
> The puffed, and bid the masker strip,
> And into the crowned windbag thrust,
> Tearing the mortal from the vital thing,
> A lightning o'er the half-illumed. . . .

In these thirteen lines the Comic Spirit, to which the
passage is addressed, is engaged in an extraordinary
variety of occupations, from cleaning paths to playing
lightning. Its victims are to be the clipped, plumed,
and puffed, stripped maskers, punctured wind-bags,
kings exhibited in their naked manhood, dull-eyed
mortals blinded by lightning. The eighth and ninth

lines show us a characteristic telescoping of metaphors, two entirely different ones being joined together by the verb "clip", which is used in two different senses. We are told that the "oversteppings" of the plumed are to be clipped, that is, their movements are to be restricted. But the choice of "clip" and "the plumed" suggests too that their finery is to be sheared away. "Portmanteau" metaphors of this kind are very common in Meredith; and passages in which the imagery is even more crowded and involved than it is here would not be difficult to find.

For a mind that works in this fashion, poetry, it would seem, with its swift movement, its indifference to logical development, and so forth, is the right form. It is obvious that prose written in this manner will be a kind of ugly duckling. Yet it is doubtful if the method is not more successful in a kind of swift poetical prose than it is in poetry proper. The trouble is that the reader's imagination is not allowed to enjoy the images offered to it, but must, as it were, immediately throw them over to the intellect. It is highly necessary that the images should not be fully and intensely realised, otherwise they clash with one another and the effect Meredith intended is lost. The result of this is a lack of the sensuous element in the poetry, and the reader's imagination cannot help feeling starved. Here again is a reason why so many persons, who constantly read verse and are not unaccustomed to subtle thought subtly expressed, find so much of Meredith's verse obscure and "difficult". Not only, as we have seen, is there little appeal to the ear, but the imagination is also denied the satisfaction of enjoying a succession of concrete rounded images. Writing of this kind seems

witty rather than what we would usually call poetical.
When a metaphor is allowed to remain present to the
mind some time before another thrusts it out, or when
the images can be fully explored without any loss, the
effect of this manner is very bold and striking and may
be extremely beautiful.   Things can be adequately
presented that are beyond the reach of a more formal
style.   An example of this can be found in a passage
in "The Sage Enamoured":

> Look in, she said, as pants the furnace, brief,
> Frost-white. She gave his hearing sight to view
> The silent chamber of a brown curled leaf:
> Thing that had throbbed ere shot black lightning through.
> No further sign of heart could he discern:
> The picture of her speech was winter sky;
> A headless figure folding a cleft urn,
> Where tears once at the overflow were dry. . . .

And many of the best things in "Modern Love"
owe their excellence, indeed their unique quality, to
this bold use of metaphor.   It is perhaps significant
that both these poems are unusual not only in their
manner, but also in their matter, both being subtle
narratives or psychological studies, and, indeed, simply
Meredith novels given to us in essence.   And even
with these poems, which we probably do not read in
the way that we read ordinary lyrical verse, this use of
metaphor is only partly successful. It gives us moments
of unique force and beauty, but when those moments
are not present we are apt to descend from poetry to
a kind of agonised or turgid wit, and sometimes from
that to what can only be considered the wreck and
ruin of the English style.

Something similar might be said of Meredith's
poetry as a whole.   He brings to the work good qualities

enough to equip two ordinary poets. At the same time he has faults enough to prevent almost any other man from ever being a poet at all. His poetry has everything but decent mediocrity. He offers us everything, from passages of the utmost force and beauty to the very lava and ashes of language, except pleasant tepid exercises in verse-making. If sheer originality, a highly personal way of thinking, and writing, is the criterion, then he must be regarded as one of the greatest poets we have had, for it would be difficult to find a larger body of original thought and a more personal voice than his. On any other test he must be given a much lower place. He is a considerable poet, but only a great poet at moments. These moments give him greatness because of that originality of his. When he does blaze and hack his way through to beauty, it is a new beauty of his own that is of the utmost value to the reader because it adds something unique to his experience. Wrestling with a body of profound and original thought, and having to create for himself a new tradition, a new set of symbols, Meredith had to work under the most difficult conditions, and these difficulties, combined with certain weaknesses we have already noted, are frequently too much for him. But when he overcomes them his triumph is all the greater. The somewhat stoical and rationalistic creed, disdaining passion as it did, he set himself to express, made his task all the harder, for passion is the friend of poets. As we have seen, it is the impelling force of emotion that we miss in so much of his work, and the lack of it is largely the secret of its weakness. As the poet of Man and Nature, his task was far more difficult than Wordsworth's, for Wordsworth, confronted by a

Nature that was for him only the veil of infinity,
another and greater reality, could at his emotional
height break through and lose himself in an apocalyptic
vision. This, by the nature of his creed, Meredith
could not do, but in the great moments had to see the
earth and the sky more clearly and truthfully than
before, only now irradiated by high emotion. And it
is the secret of the enduring appeal of his finest poetry
that it does reveal Nature, the woods and flowers and
birds and clouds all bathed in this clear golden light, as
Nature has never been revealed before by any poetry.
It brings to us an ecstasy, not of secret midnights and
a burning brain, but compounded of an honest mind
and pure daylight. The poet in such moments is like
his own skylark:

> For singing till his heaven fills,
> 'Tis love of earth that he instils,
> And ever winging up and up,
> Our valley is his golden cup,
> And he the wine which overflows
> To lift us with him as he goes. . . .

There is much in this poetry that is brackish and cloudy
with dregs, but there is too, from the eager youthful
ecstasies of "Love in the Valley", to the profound and
lovely symbolism of the "Hymn to Colour", this wine
of song, ready to restore us back to health and sanity
and then to renew old enchantments.

CHAPTER V

ONCE Meredith's view of Man and Earth is understood, it is not difficult to grasp the significance of what he calls the Comic Spirit, which is the very mainspring of his fiction. Even if he had not given us two disquisitions on the subject, one the *Essay on Comedy and the Uses of the Comic Spirit,* the other the poem entitled "Ode to the Comic Spirit", there are still several passages in the novels that would enable us to form a shrewd idea of what it meant to him. We have seen that he throws the emphasis neither upon a mechanical universe nor upon an individual soul, exiled for a term to this world from which it will have to be "saved", but upon the community of humankind, through which are being realised the purposes of Earth. Meredith first stresses the community of Man and Nature, and then the community of Man and Man. He was one of the first of those modern thinkers who throw the emphasis forward ("the rapture of the forward view"), insisting that man should concentrate upon the human society he is helping to build up, keeping before his mind not the Kingdom of Heaven and the state of his soul but the Kingdom of Earth and the happiness of his children

and his children's children. Like all men of a radical
and reforming temper, he is a social optimist and has
a definite belief in progress. Society is not perfect,
otherwise it would be in no need of reform, but, on
the other hand, it is sound at the core, representing
a very definite advance, otherwise it would not be
worth reforming, it would only be worth destroying.
There is in Meredith no corroding touch of that
pessimism which is found in so many writers of the
later nineteenth century, writers who suddenly stared
about them, having heard so much suspiciously complacent talk of progress, realised that the millennium
had not arrived, and were so disgusted that human
society was not immaculate that they wished to plunge
it into chaos. Such pessimists would themselves, in
Meredith's view, be comic figures, the rightful prey ·
of the Comic Spirit, for the shadow of their Ego is
monstrously elongated. Meredith's attitude towards
society approximates very closely to that of the philosophical reformers, idealists and English Hegelians
(who acted as marriage broker and midwife to Hegel
and the Liberal Movement), who were prominent in
Oxford and elsewhere during the third quarter of the
century. Indeed, it is possible to claim, as Mr. Basil
de Sélincourt actually does do, an idealistic basis for
Meredith's view of the Comic Spirit, transforming it
into a kind of literary supplement to the works of
T. H. Green.

We have also seen that Meredith holds a Greek
balance. He is the prophet of an ardent temperance.
Our business is to spiritualise the life of Earth, and
we can only do that by using animal energy in the
service of spirit, not by draining out our blood but by

putting it to good uses. He breaks through the time-old antithesis of spirit and sense, tossing aside ascetism and sensualism to his vultures of the Comic, and in its place substitutes the antithesis of Self and—what we might call—the larger self, of the Ego and the spirit. It is not for nothing that his most characteristic work is called *The Egoist,* for to him egoism in one form or another is the chief danger as men are now constituted. As we develop, egoism assumes more and more subtle forms, wears more and more elaborate disguises, and becomes increasingly difficult to detect. This it is, this self-absorption, this inability to face entirely outwards (where there is, in the end, the promise of real happiness), that leads men to shrink from an open commerce with facts and to take refuge in the dark holes of cynicism, sentimentalism, and the rest. It is for ever destroying the proper balance of blood, brain, and spirit that we have already noted. The mark of it is a want of proportion somewhere, and it is the natural prey of the Comic Spirit, which has a most exquisite sense of proportion and pounces upon whatever is lop-sided, bloated, stunted, or atrophied. Here is Meredith's own account of the Comic Spirit, as he gives it in his *Essay on the Idea of Comedy:*

If you believe that our civilisation is founded in common sense (and it is the first condition of sanity to believe it), you will, when contemplating men, discern a Spirit overhead; not more heavenly than the light flashed upward from glassy surfaces, but luminous and watchful; never shooting beyond them, nor lagging in the rear; so closely attached to them that it may be taken for a slavish reflex, until its features are studied. It has the sage's brows, and the sunny malice of a faun lurks at the corners of the half-closed lips drawn in an idle wariness of half tension. That slim feasting smile, shaped like the long-bow, was once a big round satyr's laugh, that flung up the brows like a fortress lifted by gunpowder. The laugh will come again, but it will be of the order of the smile, finely tempered, showing sunlight of the mind, mental richness rather than noisy enormity. Its common aspect is one of unsolicitous observation, as if surveying a full field and having leisure to dart on its chosen morsels, without any fluttering eagerness. Men's future on earth does not attract it; their honesty and shapeliness in the present does; and whenever they wax out of proportion, overblown, affected, pretentious, bombastical, hypocritical, pedantic, fantastic-ally delicate; whenever it sees them self-deceived or hoodwinked, given to run riot in idolatries, drifting into vanities, congregating in absurdities, planning short-sightedly, plotting dementedly; whenever they are at variance with their professions, and violate the unwritten but perceptible laws binding them in consideration one to another; whenever they offend sound reason, fair justice; are false in humility or mined with conceit, individually, or in the bulk—the Spirit overhead will look humanely malign and cast an oblique light on them, followed by volleys of silvery laughter. That is the Comic Spirit.

The "Ode to the Comic Spirit" strikes the same note in its opening lines:

> Sword of Common Sense!—
> Our surest gift: the sacred chain
> Of man to man: firm earth for trust
> In structures vowed to permanence:—
> Thou guardian issue of the harvest brain!

In both passages, it will be noticed, the intimate relation between the Comic Spirit and common sense is insisted upon, and it is impossible to go any further without stopping to consider what exactly is meant by "common sense".

It obviously means something more than normal

understanding, though it does not altogether recede ·
from this common definition. The fundamental
normality, itself implying a balance, is still there. It
may be taken to mean the product of that sweet
reasonableness which is the result of a certain detachment, being only possible when the world is not seen
only in the flickering illuminations of one's own desires
and aspirations, but is observed clearly, in a steady
light. Our society is rooted in this common sense,
without which it would not be possible. It is, as the
name we give it implies, common enough. But it is
only common, so to speak, at certain levels. It is apt
to disappear in persons who feel or know more than
their fellows. Once you move forward into greater
sensitiveness, into innumerable labyrinths of sensation
and emotion, you are apt to let go of this silken thread
that links you to the world. The more weight you
have to bear, the harder it is to keep a balance. The more
complicated life appears, the more difficult it is to pre-
serve a sufficient sense of proportion. When we come to
supremely sensitive persons, who are compelled to have
a very lively interest in their own Egos, imaginative
emotional persons, such as artists of all kinds, then
common sense becomes the last and greatest gift of
the gods. It is, indeed, the sign and mark of the
greatest among them. The supreme poet, the Shakespeare, has it unmistakably; minor poets have commonly not a trace of it.

Humour, real humour, is simply the combined
product of a steady, unwavering common sense and
unusual powers of imagination and feeling; the first
pounces on the incongruity, the second play round
it and end by associating themselves with the object

first assailed, thus concluding with an outburst of sympathetic laughter. "If you laugh all round him (the ridiculous person)," Meredith remarks, "tumble him, roll him about, deal him a smack, and drop a tear on him, own his likeness to you and your neighbour, spare him as little as you shun, pity him as much as you expose, it is a spirit of Humour that is moving you." This is not the Comic, which gives us "thoughtful laugher" and is "the perceptive, the governing spirit". *The Essay on the Idea of Comedy* is an astonishingly brilliant performance, the best of its kind we have, but its pronouncements no more invite a close scrutiny and analysis than did Mrs. Mountstuart Jenkinson's epigrams. There is, for example, some confusion between the informing spirit and the manner of expression. Thus, Irony is treated as if it were something more than a mode of expression and, as such, one of the instruments of the Comic Spirit. Incidentally, it is too often assumed that Meredith, in this Essay, is describing the spirit in which his own work is conceived and not discussing a literary form. In places he is, but actually his own work far transcends the limits imposed by him upon the creator of pure Comedy. (Richmond Roy, for example, is a humorous creation.) The Comic Spirit, then, unlike Humour, preserves its detachment, content to throw a beam of clear light on some incongruity. Its appeal is from common sense to common sense, from normality to normality, and it simply calls the attention to what Folly is serving up for it. It must always look on and can never associate itself with its object, except for the purpose of irony. Common sense, whatever its level may be, is clearly social sense,

and its sword, the Comic Spirit, is drawn against whatever is anti-social. Comedy, we may say, is society
protecting itself—with a smile.

This theory of Comedy as a social weapon is
Meredith's great contribution to philosophical criticism
(though, of course, comic writers had justified themselves by a very crude statement of the theory for
centuries), and it has undeniable value, but, like most
enthusiastic innovators, he makes claims that are too
sweeping. As the greater part of his Essay deals
with Comedy proper, which has always been able to
ridicule passing follies and thus has helped to exter-
minate them, his claims there are sufficiently just. An
absurd fashion of dress or speech or the like, seeking
applause but finding itself ridiculed on the Comic
Stage, perishes at a touch; and if Meredith's theory
went no further than this, it would be true, but not
exactly new. It is his larger claims that are too
sweeping, particularly those he would make for the
Comic Spirit informing his own work. He throws too
much emphasis upon its purely corrective tendencies,
more especially its power of purging fools of their folly.
There is too much talk of "the doomed quarry". If
the Comic Idea prevailed with us, he tells us, "Prosers
now pouring forth on us like public fountains would
be cut short in the street and left blinking, dumb
as pillar-posts, with letters thrust in their mouths"—
an admirable comic image, but born of a far too optimistic view of the situation. The trouble is that subtle
Comedy. throwing egoism and its antics into high
relief, will provide us with a healthy and mirthful
spectacle, but it will leave the victims exactly as it
found them, with not a shadow flitting across their

self-esteem. The young man who in Stevenson's
anecdote, read *The Egoist* and rushed off to Meredith
to reproach the amused author for drawing him as Sir
Willoughby Patterne, no doubt derived considerable
benefit from his reading of that masterpiece, but
actually he was in no great danger of becoming a
Sir Willoughby. The Patternes of this world could
read *The Egoist* for ever without the smallest crumpled
rose-petal of a doubt ever finding its way under the
nine bolsters of their self-approval. The subtle comic
writer, it would seem, is doomed to preach to the
converted, for the arrows of his wit rattle harmlessly
against the armour of the insensitive, his natural prey.
"There are plain reasons", Meredith admits in his
essay, "why the Comic poet is not a frequent appari-
tion; and why the great Comic poet remains without
a fellow. A society of cultivated men and women is
required, wherein ideas are current and the per-
ceptions quick, that he may be supplied with matter
and an audience." Great Comedy has only flourished
at a few favoured moments, when a small exclusive
society, held together by a common sense of values
that has extended upward even to the merest trifles
of conduct and appearance, has given the Comic poet
an audience to which he could appeal, perhaps with
the merest lift of an eyebrow, with every chance of
being understood. But in such a society, common
sense need wear no sword.

The mistake, in treating of the more subtle forms
of Comedy, is to stress the effect upon the victim
instead of upon the spectator. It may be said that
the spectators *are* the victims, but this is not altogether
true. The spectators are only potential victims, and

are, indeed, in no immediate danger or they would never see themselves so clearly. But they are, as it were, braced by the spectacle; their resolution to see clearly, already in existence or they would not respond to the appeal of the Comic Spirit, is strengthened; the air, hazy with lingering self-flattery and deception, is sweetened and made luminous by the fresh winds of criticism and the clear light of intellect. Comedy purges with thoughtful laughter. And Meredith comes still closer to the heart of his subject when he remarks: "You may estimate your capacity for Comic perception by being able to detect the ridicule of them you love, without loving them less: and more by being able to see yourself somewhat ridiculous in dear eyes, and accepting the correction their image of you proposes". And we may add that you may further estimate your capacity for Comic perception by being able to see your very self as a Comic figure. The Comic Spirit enables you, at certain moments, to observe yourself outside the golden haze of your desires and aspiration, as a naked figure robbed of its robes and moons and music, so that the stern grappling with yourself, arduous at any time, but most arduous, if not impossible, in a world where nothing but self-deception flourishes, is made somewhat easier. The sword of common sense is placed in your own hand. As you join in the gleeful pursuit of a Sir Willoughby, you hear the sickening patter of a hunted creature somewhere at the back of your own mind and realise that there is a tiny Sir Willoughby perishing there. Unless you yourself are associated both with the hunters and the hunted, the Comic Spirit has failed disastrously of its object, which is to purge and not

to plume its audience with a sense of their superiority.
The danger of its use among fools and the insensitive
is not merely that they will not recognise themselves
—and they will certainly not—but that they will
simply realise that a hunt is going forward, will join
in the delightful scamper, and return flushed with
triumph, more in love with themselves and more convinced of their superiority than ever. That is why
many persons dislike this talk of the Comic Spirit,
because it seems to them to breed merely a new and
more subtle kind of Pharisaism, whose Caiaphas is
Meredith himself; and it is for this reason that so
many readers, who are willing to admit his great gifts,
have a distaste both for him and his works. But such
persons are too hasty: there is a great deal in Meredith
that has escaped their notice.

The secret of Meredith is that he is himself the
principal object of his Comic perception. It would
not be difficult, as we have seen, to illumine his figure
in that "oblique light" of the Comic; there are many
passages in his life, when surveyed somewhat coldly,
that seem to ask for it; the man who could write
some of the letters and talk some of the interviews
is undeniably a ripe subject for comic treatment. Yet
there would be little satisfaction in such a treatment,
even if it were spurred on by real dislike, for the
simple reason that he himself has everywhere fore-
stalled us. Just as we are maliciously enjoying the
fact that, let us say, some passage in the letters or some
piece of reported talk recalls to us the bland accents
of Sir Willoughby Patterne, we suddenly remember
that this is, after all, the very man who created Sir
Willoughby for us and made us sensitive to such

accents. Should we turn upon Meredith and report not altogether favourably, in that dry light he extolled, upon his own life, as some critics have done, he can retort with Whitman:

I am the teacher of athletes;
He that by me spreads a wider breast than my own proves
    the width of my own;
He most honours my style who learns under it to destroy
    the teacher. . . .

He could indeed say more than this, for not only has he taught us the method, but, if he is to be the prey, he has shown us where to strike, bared back and breast. Comedy, with Meredith, begins at home. He has himself nobly entertained the Comic Spirit. It is for this reason that his finest Comedy, and particularly *The Egoist,* cuts so deep and makes it almost impossible for us to disassociate ourselves from its victims; for here there is something more than close and cruel observation, something more than a comic idea subtly transformed into flesh and blood; there is genuine self-revelation of a very curious and novel kind, one part of the self, as it were, showing up another, autobiography sketched against an ironic background. The intellect of George Meredith may be observed presenting, like a mocking showman, the temperament of George Meredith. Once, referring to the reviewers who had attacked him, he remarked: "They have always been abusing me. I have been observing them. It is the crueller process." But it was not the reviewers and their like that gave him his subtlest and most searching Comedy, for this is the result of a very different process, namely, that of both observing and abusing George Meredith. And that is a far healthier and more fruitful process.

This explains a fact that must have puzzled many readers of the novels. It explains why the characters who are wrong in those novels are so much more vital and arresting than the characters who are right. Let us admit at once that Meredith's philosophy, which forms the ground plan of his fiction, is more potent negatively than positively, is more efficacious as a rod of correction than it is as a pilgrim's staff; so that it has most force and appeal when it is attacking, when it is thrust, like the tell-tale clinical thermometer, between the lips of its victims. This partly explains why we find the latter, in contrast with the personages reported to be in good mental health, the more arresting. Also it must be remembered that the characters who are right, the philosophical heroes, the Whitfords and Redworths, being themselves the representatives of a point of view that informs the whole stories in which they appear, are always seen against a background of their own colour. If Meredith's attitude of mind, forming the background of *The Egoist,* be represented as blue in colour, then Whitford is also blue, whereas Sir Willoughby, for instance, is, let us say, a bright scarlet. Therefore, it is not surprising that the Whitfords and Redworths do not easily catch our eye and always remain a little drab and undistinguished. They have been conceived, as it were, negatively, their primary task not being to do something, but simply to avoid making the mistakes of the comic victims. It is obviously difficult to draw an arresting figure on these lines. But such personages as Vernon Whitford are not meant to be arresting figures, but are "points of rest" in the narrative, and chiefly serve as mouthpieces for the novelist's philosophy and, in a measure, as rough personifications of that philosophy.

It indicates a certain weakness in the philosophy itself that these characters so intimately connected with it should seem such dry sticks, men made out of wood, but the philosopher is, for the most part, only making his appearance here as a Comic censor, in his critical capacity, and therefore only conceives such characters in a negative spirit. Vernon Whitford, Austin Wentworth, Redworth, "Matey" Weyburn, Merthyr Powys, Dartrey Fenellan—these and their like are all excellent persons, but we cannot help feeling that they are all a trifle stiff and priggish, and not one of them seizes hold of the imagination. They are only there to be passed over, with a nod of approval, by the Comic Spirit. They are health in a hospital, where it cuts a dull figure. But though these characters may serve Meredith's philosophy in various capacities, may be its mouthpieces and so forth, there is actually very little of Meredith himself in them. There could hardly be a greater contrast between two men than there would be between Meredith and a Whitford or a Redworth. So far as he descends to a description of personal qualities in these characters—and he is apt to leave them a little abstract, as embodied points of view—such qualities seem worlds removed from anything we know of George Meredith. The characteristics that people disliked in Meredith himself are the very ones that are carefully eliminated from these "heroes", so much so that a touch of romantic nonsense, let us say a dash of Horace de Craye in Vernon Whitford, would have improved them beyond recognition. These plain stalking fellows are worlds away from the dashing epigrammatist and Olympian of Box Hill. A little comic writer always hits hardest at what is furthest from himself and, so far as he has a hero, presents us with his own features. But a great comic writer does what Meredith did, and, wanting a hero, gives us what his brain considers a sound service-able fellow, to whom the Comic Spirit offers friendship, but, wanting a victim, an awful example, a sacrifice, begins with himself. That is why he is a great comic writer.

The people who are wrong in Meredith's novels are more arresting than the people who are right, not merely because the Comic Spirit singles them out and magnifies them to us, but because they have actually more of Meredith's own self in them. Even when they are made detestable and are cruelly handled, as Sir Willoughby is, there is plain evidence that the judge has placed himself in the dock. Men of a large nature never hit so hard as when they turn upon themselves, lashing what they consider, in their wiser and cooler moments, some secret vice. They use dead selves not as stepping-stones but as whipping-boys. Vernon Whitford could not have written *The Egoist*, because he could never have seen enough. Although he was living with an egoist, he had not lived with one so intimately as George Meredith had. It strikes one as being somewhat ironical, at first, that many of the best-known quotations from Meredith should be quotations from Sir Austin Feverel's "Pilgrim's Scrip", the work of a character who is proved to be a very faulty thinker; and yet it is perhaps only just, for there is a good deal of Meredith himself even in Sir Austin Feverel. As for the delightful snobs and pretenders, such as the Countess de Saldar and Richmond Roy, they are so vitally created, towering as they do above the more sensible characters, just because there is so much of their creator's temperament in them. He can stand aside for a time to allow the Comic Spirit and its attendant imps to do their worst, but every now and then the creator in him thrusts aside the critic, the temperament of Meredith thrusts aside the intellect, and he proceeds to enjoy these characters, accepts them with romantic gusto, and succeeds in communicating that enjoyment to us. It is significant that while there were living models for the more sympathetic characters, such as Leslie Stephen for Vernon Whitford and Stevenson for Gower Woodseer, there are not even rumours of living models for the chief unsympathetic ones, as there are, for example, with Dickens, who actually worked far more wildly. There was no need of models, for Meredith, as we have said, began with himself. That is why this Comedy of his, for all its complexity, in spite of weaknesses innumerable, presses home and never fails to hit the mark at which it aims. We read on, amused, detached, secure with the philosophic showman whose fingers jerk the puppets across the stage, but suddenly the shafts are let loose, the mimic arrows lengthen and roar out into life-size bolts and are soon dealing death to our complacency. Meredithian Comedy ends by making us examine ourselves, because it is the creation of a man who began by examining his own secret self.

So far nothing has been said of Meredith's attitude towards Woman, which is closely connected with his view of the Comic. In his Essay he brings the position of Woman into intimate relation with Comedy, suggesting that one depends upon the other. In the East, he remarks, there is laughter but no Comedy, because "where the veil is over women's faces, you cannot have society, without which the senses are barbarous and the Comic Spirit is driven to the gutters of grossness to slake its thirst". And "there has been fun in Bagdad. But there never will be civilisation where Comedy is not possible; and that comes of some degree of social equality of the sexes." The higher the veil is lifted from the face of Woman and the more freely she moves among men, the greater the possibilities of Comedy. He makes this plain in an earlier passage of considerable importance:

And question cultivated women whether it pleases them to be shown moving on an intellectual level with men, they will answer that it does; numbers of them claim the situation. Now, Comedy is the fountain of sound sense; not the least perfectly sound on account of the sparkle: and Comedy lifts women to a station offering them free play for their wit, as they usually show it, when they have it, on the side of sound sense. The higher the Comedy, the more prominent the part they enjoy in it. Dorine in the *Tartuffe* is common sense incarnate, though palpably a waiting-maid. Célimène is undisputed mistress of the same attribute in the *Misanthrope;* wiser as a woman than Alceste as man. In Congreve's *Way of the World,* Millamant overshadows Mirabel, the sprightliest male figure of English Comedy.

But those two ravishing women, so copious and so choice of speech, who fence with men and pass their guard, are heartless! Is it not preferable to be the pretty idiot, the passive beauty, the adorable bundle of caprices, very feminine, very sympathetic, of romantic and sentimental fiction? Our women are taught to think so. The Agnès of the *École des Femmes* should be a lesson for men.

The heroines of Comedy are like women of the world, not necessarily heartless from being clear-sighted : they seem so to the sentimentally-reared only for the reason that they use their wits, and are not wandering vessels crying for a captain or a pilot. Comedy is an exhibition of their battle with men, and that of men with them : and as the two, however divergent, both look on one object, namely, Life, the gradual similarity of their impressions must bring them to some resemblance. The Comic poet dares to show us men and women coming to this mutual likeness ; he is for saying that when they draw together in social life their minds grow liker; just as the philosopher discerns the similarity of boy and girl, until the girl is marched away to the nursery. Philosopher and Comic poet are of a cousinship in the eye they cast on life: and they are equally unpopular with our wilful English of the hazy region and the ideal that is not to be disturbed.

Meredith's view of the relations between the sexes— and his Comedy mainly circles round these relations —is plain to see in this passage.

As everybody knows, Meredith was what is often called a feminist. Like many of the leading radicals of his time, he believed that Woman was in subjection to a man-made society, and he approved of the growing agitation in favour of her political and social freedom, even going to the length of writing a poem that is nothing more than a debate on the question. As we have seen from passages already quoted, he connects the two ideas of Comedy and Woman's status in his Essay, and there is a further passage in which the two are very sharply brought together :

I am not quoting the Arab to exhort and disturb the somnolent East ; rather for cultivated women to recognise that the Cosmic Muse is one of their best friends. They are blind to their interests in swelling the ranks of the sentimentalists. Let them look with their clearest vision abroad and at home. They will see where they have no

social freedom, Comedy is absent: where they are household drudges, the form of Comedy is primitive: where
they are tolerably independent, but uncultivated, exciting
melodrama takes its place and a sentimental version of them.
Yet the Comic will out, as they would know if they listened
to some of the private conversations of men whose minds
are undirected by the Comic Muse: as the sentimental
man, to his astonishment, would know likewise, if he in
similar fashion could receive a lesson. But where women
are on the road to an equal footing with men, in attain-
ments and in liberty—in what they have won for themselves, and what has been granted them by a fair civilisation—there, and only waiting to be transplanted from life
to the stage, or the novel, or the poem, pure Comedy
flourishes, and is, as it would help them to be, the sweetest
of diversions, the wisest of delightful companions.

Woman is the ally of the Comic Spirit, because she
has a large fund of that sweet common sense which
nourishes and sustains Comedy. She can be foolish
enough, but only, for the most part, in trifles, and is
far less likely than man to be Will-o'-the-Wisped away
by sheer unreason masquerading as reason. She is
closer to Nature, not in the sense of being less civilised
(unless the term is given a sinister meaning as it is in
the famous aphorism, "Woman will be the last thing
civilised by Man", which is an ironical stroke aimed
at its author, Sir Austin Feverel), but in the sense of
having a closer grasp of the abiding natural principles
of this life. She is nearer the earth, and her task, in
the commerce of the sexes, is to see that man is
nourishingly rooted there and not left to famish in the
mid-air of his dreams. Nature pricks her away from
egoism, so that a female Sir Willoughby is almost
unthinkable. And the thing that will almost inevitably
set her right and cause her common sense to shine more

brightly is the very thing that will tempt men to folly.
and obscure such common sense as they have, and that,
of course, is love.   In Meredith's Comedy, love is the
fool's opportunity to show himself in his true glaring
colours: it is the egoist's trap.

Love, with Meredith, is always a facing outward
and not a facing inward, a mere emotional barter; it is
a life to be lived together by two in a divine companionship.   Even in that rhapsody of early passion, "Love
in the Valley", the emphasis is thrown outward, into
a world now seen by the ecstatic lover with the dew
of Eden upon it.   We are told of Redworth and Diana:

> She gave him comprehension of the meaning of love;
> a word in many mouths, not often explained.   With her,
> wound in his idea of her, he perceived it to signify a new
> start in our existence, a finer shoot of the tree stoutly
> planted in good gross earth; the senses running their live
> sap, and the minds companioned, and the spirits made
> one by the whole-natured conjunction.   In sooth, a happy
> prospect for the sons and daughters of Earth, divinely
> indicating more than happiness: the speeding of us,
> compact of what we are, between the ascetic rocks and the
> sensual whirlpools, to the creation of certain nobler races,
> now very dimly imagined.

And for this channel between the ascetic rocks and the
sensual whirlpools, women have commonly the keener
eye and the steadier hand on the tiller.   But for this
voyage and its happy companionship, Woman needs
freedom to express herself and to disengage herself
from the sentimental image of her set up by egoistical
males.   Men often do not break the vicious circle of
self even when they love, or imagine that they love,
simply because they only fasten upon an image they
have made for themselves.   Thus they are apt to

demand what they call "purity", a total unspotting from the gross world: they are not looking for another human creature but rather a virgin white page across. which they can scrawl their names. Meredith nailed such egoistical base coinings of love to the counter for ever. He saw that if love is necessarily founded on equal rights and the companionship of minds, then many long-cherished ideas must be flung aside. Society must protect itself (there is never any trace in Meredith of the purely rebellious attitude in these as in any other matters, for such an attitude would be inconsistent with his whole philosophy), but the blow should fall equally upon the sexes: Nature tells men and women to "Share your guilt in common". To put it shortly, if Woman is to be regarded as a real person, with a present and a future, she must, if necessary, be allowed also to have had a past. The situation is examined at length in that curious poem, "The Sage Enamoured and the Honest Lady", in which the lady confesses to her philosophical middle-aged lover that she has had an unfortunate past; and the matter is touched upon in several of the novels, notably in *Rhoda Fleming* and *One of the Conquerors,* though unfortunately he never really grappled with the situation very closely in his fiction.

It is worth remembering that Meredith, like other novelists of his period, suffered from the prudery of the age. Indeed, although he was less timid than most of his contemporaries, he probably suffered more than any of them because a bold facing of the facts was an essential part of his attitude, and further because Comedy itself demands a complete frankness. An age devoted to an over-discreet and almost suffocating reticence is not likely to produce great Comedy. We have it on record that one of his friends, fearful lest Meredith should offend the public taste, spent at least one busy evening persuading him to cancel some passages in one of the earlier novels. As Meredith was not likely to have filled his pages with mere licentious talk, we can only regret that such reticence, inevitably leading to hints and obscurities and fantastic circumlocutions, should have been thought necessary. But his attitude is plain enough. He sees Woman as an individual, the mate of Man, and fastens upon and transfixes whatever in sentiment or sensuality would deny that equal individuality. Once she is no longer regarded as a possession, the sensualist's ripe fruit, the sentimentalist's nodding image, the values about her are apt to change. Chastity takes precedence of conventional purity. The clean mind is of more importance than the untarnished reputation. There are innumerable passages in Meredith in which the conventional male view of Woman is assailed and something nearer truth and beauty put in its place. Thus, in *The Amazing Marriage,* after a comparison of women and flowers, we are told:

We do homage to those ungathered, and reserve our supremacy; the gathered, no longer courted, are the test of men. When the embraced woman breathes respect into us, she wings a beast. We have from her the poetry of the tasted life; excelling any garden-gate or threshold lyrics called forth by purest early bloom. Respect for her person, for her bearing, for her character: that is in the sum a beauty plastic to the civilised young man's needs and cravings, as queenly physical loveliness has never so fully been to him along the walks of life, and as ideal worships cannot be for our nerving contentment. She brings us to the union of body and soul; as good as to say, earth and

heaven. Secret of all human aspirations, the ripeness of
the creeds, is there; and the passion for the woman
desired has no poetry equalling that of the embraced
respected woman.

In the whole range of fiction, which has constantly had
love for its theme, it would be difficult to discover any
words on the subject wiser than these. But they
represent Meredith as poet-philosopher rather than as
critic-philosopher, and there is throughout his Comedy
the spectacle of woman "winging" a beast in quite a
different sense, and a discussion of that will bring us
to the heart of Meredithian Comedy.

Meredith's women, and by that we mean the central
figures, the heroines, and not minor female characters
who may themselves be comic sketches, have a double
function just as he himself appears, in his fiction, in a
double capacity. The poet, the romancer, the creator
in him, with whom we are not immediately concerned,
lavishes all his art upon them and delights in them.
They are growing images of health and beauty, the
fruits of right living. His philosophy melts into lyric
ecstasy at the sight of them, for they are Earth, smiling
and triumphant, her very bloom and radiance. But
the critic in him uses them as a kind of test. So close
are they to Nature that, for the purposes of drama, they
actually take her place, become personifications of her.
A love story in Meredith is as much a love story, that
is, an account of the intimate relationship between a
man and a woman, as a love story in any other fiction,
but it is nearly always something else as well, an
illustration, in terms of human relationships, of the
clash of different philosophies and attitudes of mind.
The direct statements of the poetry are dramatised in

the fiction. And as nearly all his comic victims are men whose egoism has led them away from Nature into some blind alley of pride and foolishness, their attitude towards Woman, the envoy of Nature at their elbow, and their adventures in love, are deeply significant. It is when the Woman appears on the scene, setting the fantastic machinery in motion, that the Comic Spirit takes out its tablets. She becomes the test, the touchstone. This can be well illustrated by a quotation from *The Amazing Marriage,* a late novel in which Meredith spoke out rather more directly than he did in his earlier fiction. Gower Woodseer has been explaining to Fleetwood that Lady Fleetwood, having suffered a sort of kidnapping when she was bearing her child, has now a distrust of her lord and master, an inevitable state of mind, Gower tells his companion, explained in a book by an Edinburgh doctor. Then follows—

"Such animals these women are! Good Lord!" Fleetwood ejaculated. "I marry one, and I'm to take to reading medical books!" He yawned.

"You speak that of women and pretend to love Nature," said Gower. "You hate Nature unless you have it served on a dish by your own cook. That's the way to the mad-house or the monastery. There we expiate the sin of sins. A man finds the woman of all women fitted to stick him in the soil, and trim and point him to grow, and she's an animal for her pains! The secret of your malady is, you've not yet, though you're on a healthy leap for the practices of Nature, hopped to the primary conception of what Nature means. Women are in and of Nature. . . ."

And a later echo of Gower's voice, which is unmistakably the voice of Meredith himself, states the matter even more directly:

And Mr. Philosopher argues that the abusing of woman proves the hating of Nature; names it "the commonest insanity, and the deadliest", and men are "planted in the bog of their unclean animal condition until they do proper homage to the animal Nature makes the woman be. . . . Men hating Nature are insane. Women and Nature are close. If it is rather general to hate Nature and maltreat women, we begin to see why the world is a mad world. . . ."

In this story, it will be remembered, Fleetwood, in his pride and folly, deserts and ignores his Carinthia and is infuriated because her pursuit makes him look ridiculous, but he ends by pursuing her far more frantically himself, trampling down his fear of ridicule, making himself a spectacle for the gods, and all to no purpose. Broadly speaking, this may be said to be the pattern of Meredithian Comedy, repeated with endless minor variations. It might be called, in the old-fashioned manner of the pamphlets, "The Self-Coddler sent out Naked, or Nature's Revenge through the Hand of a Woman". Too tender with himself and fearing a blow to his self-esteem, a certain man will not come to terms with the facts of this life, and, shrinking from the first cutting blast of reality outside, he remains cosily in the warm and tapestried chamber of delusion and unreason. But before he has done, he has been sent out naked into the hail and east wind, his cosy chamber a gaping ruin with its shreds of tapestry flapping in the rain. He would not face a little hurt, the first shivering contact with reality, so now he must submit to a great one and be blown about and frozen. It is Love that brings about this ordeal. It is Woman who lets in the roaring winds and finally casts him out into the night.

The light of the Comic Spirit is usually focussed upon one man, always the central figure of the Comedy; and for whose sake it exists, and this light is directed there by the hand of a woman. That is the general plan of Meredith's Comedy. Sometimes, however, Woman is used as a test of or ray of illumination upon a whole group of figures. Thus, in *Sandra Belloni*, the heroine Emilia brings out, in various ways, all the people with whom she comes into contact, and lights up for us all the Pole family and their circle. To us looking on, she is something more than Emilia, the beautiful young Italian singer; she is a standard, a criterion, a value, beauty and goodness, Nature, Earth, an idealised norm. Yet she remains in the action as Emilia, an individual, one out of a number of characters in a narrative. She has a double function, as an individual (who is intensely imagined and loses nothing of her individuality) and as a kind of value, being at one and the same time a figure in the foreground and an illumination in the background. It is the successful working of this double function that gives Meredith's Comedy, at its best, its unique combination of intellectual subtlety and dramatic power. But even in *Sandra Belloni* most light is thrown upon one man, her lover, Wilfred Pole, whose sentimentalism has marked him down as the prey of the Comic Spirit; and it is his relation to Emilia that throws into bold relief his native weakness. In most of the other novels the comedy circles more narrowly round one male figure, but even in them, Woman is used as a more or less general test or illumination. Throughout she is the unconscious ambassadress of Nature. This is her place in the Comedy, where she serves as the ally of the

Comic Spirit, but this must not blind us to her individuality as one of the characters in the fiction. The
terms Comedy and fiction are not synonymous here, for
the Comedy is the comic intellectual conception that
forms the basis and directs the action of most of the
novels, whereas the fiction is made up of the novels themselves, the actual narratives, and contains, as we shall
see, numerous elements of romance, humour, tragedy,
entirely outside the scope of Comedy. As our present
business is with the latter, we are emphasising the place
of Woman in the Comedy, in which she may thus appear
as something of an abstraction; but this is only because
we are really dealing in abstractions, with the intellectual background: the actual warm and breathing
women of the fiction remain untouched.

As poet and philosopher, creator and critic, Meredith
is unmistakably the friend of Woman, who has in him
one of her most notable champions among men of letters.
Yet it is easy to exaggerate his feminism, and a good
many enthusiastic feminists, noisily enlisting him in
their ranks, might begin to feel a little dubious if they
examined his work more closely. He always surveys
the world, and Woman in that world, from a strictly
masculine angle. He asks for more freedom for Woman
in order that her common sense and native health of
mind might have more influence, and, in addition,
that she may have the opportunity of casting aside the
sentimentality into which she is so frequently entrapped,
and of gaining mental courage and strength. She will
then be the fit mate of poetic and philosophic males.
Never in his heart does he depart from the view that
the end of Woman is mating, and the goal he always
sets her is a satisfying personal relationship: "He for

God only, she for God in him". Man is here to
serve, to cherish, prune and trim, the world, and Woman
is here to serve, to cherish, prune and trim, the creature
Man. We watch his women escaping their bondage,
unmasking and thrusting aside (if they are lucky)
their egoists and sentimentalists, only to become the
wives of strenuous philosophers. However great their
courage and agile their wit, it is never suggested that
they are self-sufficient or even partially self-sufficient,
content to serve the world and express themselves in
virginal freedom; their search is simply the old search
for the right man. Clara Middleton and Lord
Ormont's Aminta have wit enough to discover the
difference between nosegays and fetters and have
courage enough to escape, but they do not escape into
the wide world but to the sides of their Whitfords and
Weyburns, and, once there, we know that they will
act in the old feminine way, listening, wide-eyed and
happy, to the staccato aphorisms of their lords, and
merely exerting a little feminine pressure when a
masculine absurdity shows signs of inflation. Even
Diana, that clipper on the high seas, has to return at
last to the harbour of Redworth. But Diana is different
from the rest of Meredith's heroines and deserves a
word to herself.

Once it is approached as something more than the
picturesque, romantic narrative that has made it the
most popular of Meredith's novels, the story of Diana
Warwick becomes somewhat baffling. This is mainly
because Meredith was himself confused, trying to do
too many things at once. In the first place, he took
from Mrs. Norton's history a number of facts that left
him either too much or too little scope for invention

(a matter to be dealt with later when we come to the
fiction proper); in the second place, he tried to make
Diana the central figure, the victim, of the Comedy,
while he also made her the heroine of the romance.
She is to be the prey of the Comic Spirit and also
Woman, its ally. It is almost as if he had tried to write
a story in which Clara Middleton and Sir Willoughby
Patterne became one and the same person. His intention was undoubtedly to write a Comedy that should
have a woman, a very brilliant and beautiful and
altogether unusual woman, as its central figure instead
of a man, but, having once created her, the poet in
him, deeply enamoured, kept shouldering the critic on
one side and, fired by a glance from her bright eyes,
told him to take up arms not against this exquisite
creature but against society in her cause. This confusion runs throughout the narrative, but its ground
plan is certainly a Comedy in Meredith's usual manner.
Woman, in Diana, takes the centre of the stage, acting
independently in the full light of the Comic, or what
would have been the full light of the Comic had not
chivalry dimmed it and given it poetic colouring. She
is no longer Woman seen in relation to a man but
seen independently, as the arbiter of her own fortunes.
Her weakness is a mingling of vanity, self-centredness,
and infirmity of will, and her misfortunes are as much
the natural result of her frailties as the mishaps of
Sir Willoughby and the others are the result of theirs.
Her ridiculous marriage with Warwick, her ill-con-
sidered friendship with Lord Dannisburgh, her reckless
extravagance and its train of debts, her betrayal of
Dacier's secret, all these have their roots in her vanity
and instability, and the misfortunes they bring are of

her own seeking. The only hope for her is to ally
herself with a stout sensible male, and him she finds
in Redworth, who will give her stability and direction.
The inference is that, in spite of her unusual qualities
of mind and heart, she was not fit to travel alone in
this world. And although the story that frames her
contains perhaps more feminism than any of the other
novels, yet, ironically enough, Diana herself is perhaps
more successful as a bad example, a hint of warning,
than she is as a good one, a sketch of free womanhood.
We have encountered her vanity and restlessness and
instability very frequently during the forty years that
have elapsed since her first appearance. It is doubtful
if a hint of this escaped the social critic in Meredith, in
spite of all the romantic rhapsodising of the poet in him
over his radiant Diana.

Perhaps the shortest approach to the comprehension
of Meredith's Comedy, or indeed any real Comedy,
is by way of Horace Walpole's favourite aphorism:
"The World is a Comedy to those who think, a Tragedy
to those who feel". Meredith made Comedy the
basis of his fiction because he chose to present life
first in terms of the intellect. He came to it first as a
thinker, who saw men and women against a background of thought, who applied to their talk and action
certain intellectual standards, who kept his mind fixed
upon what he considered to be the requisite balance
in man's nature and was therefore quick to detect any
deviation from it, any incongruity; and the result was
Comedy. His whole philosophy, as we have seen,
would urge him towards Comedy, because, in the first
place, that philosophy gives the highest place to the
intellect ("Intellect should be our aim"), which is the

chosen instrument of Comedy, and, in the second place,
it is essentially a philosophy of balance, sanity, the
golden mean, merely heightening that common sense
which is itself the basis of Comedy. In his talk, and
here and there in his poetry, Meredith was inclined
to exaggerate his brain-worship and was apt to forget
that feeling must broaden and deepen to keep pace
with the intellect, but his actual fiction sometimes rises
to sheer romance, broadens into humour, and deepens
into tragedy. It is not pure Comedy, even *The Egoist*
is not pure Comedy, but its primary conception is
Comic. The ground-plan throughout is Comedy. The
Comic Spirit presides there as it does in the pure
Comedy for the stage, examined by Meredith in his
Essay, but it is now informed not merely by common
sense but by a definite philosophy, stated in the poetry
but shown in action in the fiction. Meredith does
with fiction what Carlyle did with history. Actually
there are distinct traces of Carlyle's influence in
Meredith's earlier novels (though both owned a common influence—Jean Paul Richter), and when the two
men met, after Carlyle and his wife had read *Richard
Feverel* and liked it, Carlyle told Meredith that he ought
to write history, but Meredith, though sensible of the
compliment, was wise enough to see that he could more
successfully show his philosophy in action by means of
his development of the novel.

While he is apparently ambling, by most devious
routes, into the ordinary narrative of English fiction,
he is really seating his readers in a Greek theatre,
clearing the stage and erecting the various machines
that will carry his gods and imps of the Comic, a
mythology necessary where there should be signs of

destiny and doom. His characters move against a
philosophic background, and it is the reality of this
background, of the standards by which they come to be
doomed or saved, or of the laws by which they doom
or save themselves, that matters most to him, and not,
as with most novelists, the verisimilitude of his actual
narrative. That is why his stories have a curiously
timeless and abstract air, and why so many of the
characters in them, the figures in the middle distance,
have the unreality of old theatrical types; that is why
so many of his narratives abound in loose ends and
fantastic knots, and why after they have mounted to
one last great scene they then collapse as if the hand
directing their puppets had suddenly loosed its grasp
on the wires. Yet there move in the foreground a
certain number of characters who have something
more than the air of reality with which the ordinary
accomplished novelist can invest his people. These
characters are at once the centre of an elaborate philosophical Comedy, in which pride and folly and faulty
thinking are sapped and mined and finally blown sky-
high, and the centre of a romantic story, filled with
music and bloom and radiance, that will not allow us
to detach ourselves completely from its figures. The
romantic interest, occasionally intensified by bursts of
lyric ecstasy unique in prose fiction, compels us to feel
with these characters, to identify ourselves with them,
while the intellectual background against which they
move, with its suggestion of the Greek theatre, its gods
and imps of the Comic who control the circumstance
and fashion the doom of the unconscious mortals,
keeps its hold upon our minds and compels us to follow
the searchlight of the Comic Spirit with a philosophic

eye. Thus we achieve that curious dichotomy, self
turning to examine self, which Meredith himself
achieved when he began to create this Comedy. He
may be said to have invented a new and paradoxical
kind of literature, Romantic Comedy, which must not
be confused with so-called "romantic comedies" in
which intellectual Comedy is entirely absent, such
as those later plays of Shakespeare that are simply
romantic drama containing passages of humour. Like
his great contemporary Thomas Hardy, Meredith gave
a new turn to fiction: we might say, in the manner
of Polonius, that Meredith opposes the lyrical-comical
to Hardy's epical-tragical. How far he was successful
we shall see when we come to consider his fiction more
closely, and we need not be surprised to come upon
more than one failure, for he was engaged in a high and
even desperate enterprise. To understand to the full
the nature of that enterprise it has been necessary to
disengage his attitude, his conception of Man and
Earth and, emerging from that, his idea of the Comic
Spirit; and now having accomplished this, it is a simple
and natural step forward to the work itself. One
represents the aim and the other the achievement,
and having disengaged and, however flickeringly,
illuminated the aim, we can proceed to measure the
achievement.

CHAPTER VI

HIS FICTION: ITS FORM AND SCOPE

WE have said that Meredith gave a new turn to fiction when he brought to it what we have chosen to call his Romantic Comedy. He contrived to press the Novel into his service, and there could be no better proof of the extraordinary adaptability of the Novel than the fact that Meredith was able to make use of it at all. When he produced his *Ordeal of Richard Feverel,* the English Novel had been put to various uses, had been twisted this way and that by such writers as Scott, Jane Austen, Dickens, Thackeray, and the Brontës, who gave to romantic dreams the stamp of solid reality or carried away the real world into the atmosphere of wild romance, and produced fiction as various as their distinct and marked personalities. But different as they are, these great novelists are alike in this, that they are all narrators. Their characters may be using a dirk in the Highlands or using a teaspoon at Highbury, but they are all taking their places in a story, a definite chronicle. Meredith differs from all these novelists in that he is not, by nature or by inclination, a narrator, and hardly pretends to tell a story. Wilde's remark about Meredith, that "as a novelist he can do everything, except tell a story", is a shrewd thrust.

If you regard the Novel as a tale pure and simple, an arresting and convincing chronicle of events, then Meredith must inevitably appear a colossal failure. Few men who have put their names to a series of intelligent novels have shown less concern for the art of narration. He deliberately flouts it, and his later work is worse in this respect than his earlier. "The unspeakable *Lord Ormont*", moaned Henry James, perhaps our supreme master in the art of narration, ". . . not a difficulty met, not a figure presented, not a scene constituted—not a dim shadow condensing once either into audible or visible reality—making you hear for an instant the tap of its feet on the earth." His "critical rage", as he calls it, is easily understood: Henry James reading *Lord Ormont* is a master of fence looking on in a slaughter-house.

Regarded as a narrative, every novel that Meredith wrote is not merely faulty but downright bad, even perverse in its badness, and could be overwhelmed by adverse criticism. The movement is lame and awkward; there are loose ends everywhere; no effort is made to make events of the utmost importance to the story in any way convincing; proportion, balance, sound construction are everywhere wanting. A thousand examples of such weakness leap to the mind. *Richard Feverel* is presented as a comedy, and has a tragic ending thrust upon it, quite arbitrarily. The involved action of *Evan Harrington* will not stand the slightest examination, and the whole business of the Cogglesby brothers is preposterous. The movement of *Sandra Belloni*, clumsy enough even when left to itself, is held up by the unnecessary disquisitions of "The Philosopher"; and the relations between the impossible Mrs. Chump and the Poles, on which so much of the action turns, are never credible. *Vittoria,* avowedly a novel of incident, shows us no large lines of construction at all, and we have to make the most of individual scenes without knowing quite how we have arrived at them or where they will lead us. In *Rhoda Fleming,* Rhoda's desire that her sister should marry Sedgett, Hackbut's theft of the gold, and a host of minor matters, are all incredible, and make the latter part of the novel resemble a wild dream. After the first half of its course is run, the story in *Harry Richmond* goes to pieces; the great scene near the end that brings the Squire and Richmond Roy together is only achieved after Meredith has taxed his readers' credulity and loyalty to the uttermost; and the conclusion is a flat anti-climax only relieved by a tragic incident that is itself perilously near bathos. The construction in *Beauchamp's Career* is actually better than most of its critics would seem to imagine, but its ending is a mere huddling of the personages off the stage when their great scene is over. Even the action of *The Egoist,* though it is more tightly and carefully constructed than any of the other novels, will not stand examination. Thus, for example, there is no reason whatever, beyond the fact that there would be no drama without it, why Sir Willoughby, having missed Clara Middleton, should feel himself compelled at all cost to obtain the hand of Laetitia Dale, on which the whole climax of the story depends. There were other and easier ways of saving his vanity, or, at least, there would have been if Sir Willoughby had existed, as he does not exist, in a world something like this one. Of the remaining novels, *Diana of the Crossways, One of our Conquerors,*

Lord Ormont and his Aminta, and *The Amazing Marriage,* it need only be said that all the faults of the previous novels, the unsteady progression, the tale standing still and then taking a huge leap forward, the introduction of incredible events and unmotived actions (such as Diana's marriage with Warwick or the appearance of the baby in *The Amazing Marriage*) to play an important part in the narrative, the dallying at length with matters that contribute nothing to the story (such as the business about Durance and his serial in *One of our Conquerors*), the flat conclusions, all these faults are more in evidence than they were before. It would be wearisome to pile·up examples of what must be obvious to any reader of Meredith. He must be regarded as one of the worst narrators in the history of the English Novel.

This lack not merely of the born story-teller's gift but even of any ordinary skill in planning and setting out a narrative is undoubtedly a serious defect. Even when we realise that Meredith's aims were different from those of his fellow novelists, that he deliberately widened the scope of the Novel, it remains a serious defect, for the Novel, no matter what new purpose it may serve and what new material it may take in, must always remain a tale. It would have been an absolutely fatal defect had not Meredith had different aims, had he not given a new turn to fiction. He brought to the art a mind that seems curiously unfitted for it, both highly poetical and deeply philosophical and critical, and appearing at once too poetical and too critical and wanting in all those middle qualities that would seem to make up the mind of the novelist. Such a mind, if it was to express itself in fiction at all, could only do so

by fashioning for itself a new form. This is what
Meredith did. Already, in considering his idea of the
Comic, the Comedy that serves as the basis of his
fiction, we have had at least a glimpse of this new form
and have even given it a name, Romantic Comedy. It
is the Novel turned "lyrical-comical". It can be
considered a blend of two amazingly different elements
that correspond to the two sides, the poetical and
critical sides, of Meredith's mind. What he does is
to graft Artificial Comedy, of the kind he celebrated
in his Essay, upon highly romantic narrative. Had he
lived in another age, he might have written for the
theatre, though it is doubtful if in any age he would
have written successfully for it. But he always wrote,
as it were, for an imaginary theatre of the mind. The
Comedy that he embodied in his fiction contains all the
elements of the finest intellectual Comedy for the stage.
He was, however, a poet, as well as a philosopher and
critic, and the poet in him seeks relief too in the fiction,
with the result that the Comedy is blended with pure
romance, rising to a lyrical ecstasy that has never been
approached by any novelist before or since. With this
key we can unlock all his doors.

It is the business of the Comedy, whose significance,
scope, and movement we have already examined, to
set in motion an involved action that will exhibit the
mingled motives of the personages concerned, and to
move always towards a climax, a highly dramatic scene
in which the narrator will bring the chief characters
together, leaving them with us and retiring himself into
the background, when ironic circumstance will fasten
upon the chief victims in the manner we have already
discussed. The movement is inevitably towards a

scene of this description. Without such scenes, the
Comedy is lost, failing in its purpose; it is there to
create them, and has them in mind from the beginning.
But what of the lyric poet who has taken a hand in this
fiction? He too is clearly bound to be a man of scenes,
of heightened moments, when he can attend to his
proper task of expressing a state of mind, describing
a world, in a moment of ecstasy, bathed in light and
colour, moving to strange music, glowing with enchantments. The general conduct of the narrative is nothing
to him; not for him the necessary exposition, the
marshalling of significant facts, the shuffling of characters; but he will single out certain moments, it may
be an early morning meeting of two young lovers, the
sight of a cherry-tree in blossom, a dawn in the
mountains, and make them his own. He too moves
inevitably away from a flowing narrative to an unusual
moment, an outstanding situation, a scene. The whole
movement, then, of this fiction must be towards scenes;
and that, of course, is precisely its character. Meredith,
as all his critics have remarked, is pre-eminently the
novelist of great scenes.

He himself saw something of this. Writing to an
American critic who had just published an article on
his work, he observes: "My method has been to
prepare my readers for a crucial exhibition of the personae, and then to give the scene in the fullest of their
blood and brain under stress of a fiery situation. . . .
In the Comedies, and here and there where a concentrated presentment is in design, you will find a 'pitch'
considerably above our common human; and pur-
posely, for only in such manner could so much be
shown. Those high notes and condensings are aban-

doned when the strong human call is heard—I beg you
to understand merely that such was my intention."
There is actually far more substance in these remarks
than there is in the not infrequent references to his
method, to "philosophical fiction", that are to be
found scattered about in the novels themselves. The
Comedy is there not to produce a narrative but, whenever possible, a scene, that "crucial exhibition of the
personae" mentioned above. That is the plain difference, in method, between Meredith and most of our
other novelists. They too, unless they present us with
the simple flowing narrative that we get in Defoe,
must give us scenes, passages in which the novelist
ceases to be a chronicler and becomes a stage-manager,
for such scenes represent the high lights of the picture.
Thus when Thackeray reaches a very dramatic moment
in his *Vanity Fair* and wishes to show us Rawdon
Crawley's discovery of his wife and Steyne, he drops
his usual panoramic method, that of a man searching
through a vast haze of memory and reporting on what
he finds there, and gives us a piece of pure drama, a
scene. But the scene remains with these novelists as
nothing more than a device for heightening the
dramatic interest of the tale, as the high light in the
picture: it exists for the sake of the narrative. But
with Meredith, the narrative really exists for the sake
of the scene; it is there to hurry us from one scene
to another, to bring about the necessary complicated
action that will make a scene possible. Then, and not
until then, can the Comedy, which in a greater or less
degree is the basis of all these novels, exhibit itself.

This explains why Meredith, with all his genius and
his long acquaintance with the novel form, should be

such a weak and faulty narrator. He did not see his material as the ordinary novelist sees his. His aim is quite different. He is a faulty narrator because narrative does not interest him. What he wishes to do is not to present us with an arresting and convincing chronicle of events, but to move from one scene to another as quickly and easily as possible. Nearly all his critics have remarked upon his weak endings, novel after novel collapsing almost like punctured balloons, and have set it down to a flagging of the novelist's energy and interest at the conclusion of a long and difficult piece of work. But it is not the length and arduousness of the work that has gone before that have caused this flagging of interest, but the simple fact that, in practically all the novels, the last great scene is over and done with, the Comedy has reached its greatest height and has nothing more to do, and the novelist, who has, after all, pledged himself to write a story, is left with the task of rounding it off, a task that interests him so little that he performs it either perfunctorily or with a touch of impish perversity. It is, as we saw in the last chapter, as if the hand directing the puppets had suddenly loosened its grasp on the wires. A writer who is engaged upon a genuine tale has a very natural and strong desire to bring it to a satisfactory conclusion: he must, as it were, "see everybody home". But Meredith is not so engaged, and once he has shown his chief characters "in the fullest of their blood and brain under stress of a fiery situation" he has done with them. We might say that he has no wish to see his people home, because he knows that they are creatures of intellectual Comedy, who exist in a kind of mid-air, and therefore have no homes.

Of all Meredith's novels, *The Egoist* is generally and rightly considered the strongest. Several of the others have in them material as rich, perhaps richer, but they do not leave the same impression of strength and brilliance. There is more than one reason for this, but not the least of the reasons is that *The Egoist* is more carefully planned. It is deliberately designed as a Comedy; the novel form being the merest framework. It is as if Meredith had arrived for the first time at a definite idea of what he had been trying to do, more or less unconsciously, ever since he had turned novelist. Influenced, no doubt, by contemporary novelists who shared with their public a taste for huge sprawling narratives (creatures born of the monthly part), Meredith had so far flung himself into stories that covered comparatively long stretches of time, many changes of place, and involved a large number of minor characters, panoramic stories that demanded just that art of narrative to which he was indifferent and through which his Comedy was hardly able to struggle. Such narratives gave the romantic poetical half of him opportunities that he took good care not to miss; but the Comedy, necessitating a close design, was almost buried. In *The Egoist,* however, he plotted with some craft. Once the exposition, still rather clumsy, is done with, the novel becomes a stage set for Comedy. One scene swiftly follows another. Long intervals of time and frequent changes of place are both swept away; the action is tight and its movement rapid and inevitable; and the ending, with its significant chapter-heading, "The Curtain Falls", avoids the usual flat descent into perfunctory narrative. In this one novel, Meredith, working at last with his eyes open, no longer

VI   HIS FICTION: ITS FORM AND SCOPE   153

seeking an uneasy compromise between what he really wanted to do and what he thought a novelist ought to do, really made the form his own. The new turn he gave to fiction was completed.

Not only was the *The Egoist* deliberately written as a Comedy, set in the lightest possible framework of ordinary narrative, but from the first it imposes itself as a Comedy upon its readers. Long before we have considered the matter critically, we find ourselves regarding *The Egoist* as something quite different from the ordinary novel. That is why the criticism passed, in the earlier part of this chapter, on its action really carries no weight. It was suggested then that the central situation of the Comedy, that of Willoughby, seeing himself jilted by Clara, saving his vanity at all cost by obtaining the hand of Laetitia, is really a false one. If this alternative of Clara-Laetitia were not pressed home, there would, of course, be no sting in the concluding part of the Comedy. A Willoughby who existed in this world, or any world like it, would have escaped this alternative, never dreaming of paying the price Laetitia demanded (or probably even of offering himself there) when he lived in a county only too full of young ladies ready to accept him. He could have cherished his self-conceit to the bitter end, as our actual Sir Willoughbys always do. But actually, when we rise from the book, this line of criticism never suggests itself to us; it does not occur to us, while we are still under the spell of the Comedy, that Sir Willoughby would or could have done anything else. The alternative is inevitable; if not Clara, then it must be Laetitia. Why, assuming that our imagination has been captured by the book (there are people who never enter its atmosphere), should we feel this? Is it not simply because we are spectators of an intellectual Comedy, which always presents to us a few broad types of humanity and contrives to suggest to us that it has thus emptied the world, that the personages on the stage before us are all the people on earth? Thus there *are* no other young ladies to whom Sir Willoughby might fly, and when he acts as if there were no alternative but Laetitia, we never think, while the Comedy holds us, that he could do anything else. If we met the same situation in Shakespeare, or in the novels of Dickens or Thackeray or Hardy, it would not impose itself upon us, simply because these works are not only crowded with people who are there but also with the suggested presence of whole populations who are not there; they approximate, in this respect at least, to the real world. Turn to Molière or Congreve, or highly artificial Comedy anywhere, and immediately you find, as in *The Egoist,* a few distinct characters who move in an empty space or, if you will, in a little world that contains no one else. Comedy demands such conditions, and thus *The Egoist,* widely different as its form may appear, is only in the tradition.

In no other novel do we find the narrative so entirely at the service of the Comedy (by which we mean not the actual work but the Comic Idea) as it is in *The Egoist.* Comedy is present in all of them, but it struggles with other elements; and nowhere else is Meredith so single-minded as he is in his most famous and characteristic novel. At the other extreme there stands *Harry Richmond,* a novel that has been placed by more than one critic at the head of all Meredith's fiction. But anyone who singles this novel out for

special praise and favour is really declaring his dislike
for the form of fiction that Meredith made his own, for
though no one else could have written *Harry Richmond,*
its good qualities being all native to the writer, it is in
some respects one of his least characteristic productions.
It is really an experiment.   The fact that, unlike any
of the other novels, it is written in the first person, in
the sprawling autobiographical form that plays such a
notable part in English fiction, is significant.   It means
that the writer is about to part company with a number
of his most familiar devices.   The detachment demanded by intellectual Comedy is clearly impossible
when one of the chief actors is himself the narrator
and we are to see everything through his eyes.   Something can be done indirectly, by means of irony; while
Harry Richmond is romanticising, it may be possible
to let in Comedy, as it were, by the back door; but
the difficulties are almost insuperable.   Meredith undoubtedly planned it as a fresh departure, an experiment in the *picaresque,* in which the purely romantic
strain, never absent long from any of the novels, not
even from *The Egoist,* that was as much a part of him
as the Comic, should have full play.   But he could
not resist the temptation to make this romantic autobiography a Comedy as well.

The result is a curious mingling of atmospheres.
Meredith undoubtedly saw possibilities of Comedy in
Richmond Roy and his lordly impostures.   He might
have written another book in which Richmond Roy
was the Comic victim.   But, unfortunately, the romance
(and all the earlier chapters of the book are pure
romance and could hardly be anything else) claims
Richmond Roy for itself long before the Comedy can

make its appearance. We see him as a figure of humour; indeed he is Meredith's greatest humorous character. Comedy demands detachment, as we have seen, and this detachment cannot be achieved in the instance of Richmond Roy. We see him through the eyes of his admiring young son, and though we may dislike the kind of thing for which he stands, we find it impossible to dislike him. He is at once laughable and lovable, and thus becomes a humorous character. (It is obvious too that Meredith himself could not be detached, but threw himself into the creation of this figure with such gusto, put so much of his hidden self into him, that he is tremendously and vitally alive, in spite of his monstrous absurdities.) In order that romance should merge into Comedy, it is necessary that Harry Richmond should become gradually dis-illusioned, that Richmond Roy should play what is really a detestable part in the action; and in the later part of the story, Meredith uses all his energy and ingenuity to bring about this end, to set the Comedy in motion. But though Harry is disillusioned, we, the readers, are not, and persist in our view of Richmond Roy as a humorous character, a lovable and absurd creature to be welcomed with shouts of joy even if he wrecks the fortunes of all the people in the narrative. Thus it is Harry and his story that suffer. This explains why so many readers are left puzzled and resentful, complaining of the harsh treatment of Richmond Roy. The two opposing elements, Comedy and romance, have not been successfully united.

The autobiographical form in which this novel, and this novel alone, is cast suggests that Meredith's weak-ness in narration will not be so apparent here, because

the story is, willy-nilly, unified by the "I" who tells
it, all its incidents being at last held together by the
single memory that contains and presents them.   He
may jump from scene to scene as usual, but now he has
to take Harry Richmond with him and has to explain
how he arrived there.   The form compels him to slow
up the action and join together most of his customary
loose ends.   This partly explains (and romance and
Richmond Roy supply all other explanation necessary)
why this story has found so much favour, particularly
with those who dislike Meredith's fiction in general.
And yet this too is an affair of great scenes.   Few of us
could say, off-hand, what the story is all about, but its
heightened moments remain undimmed in the memory.
Who could forget, having once read, that opening scene
at midnight at the door of Riversley Grange, that of
the two runaway schoolboys in the London fog, that
of the bronze statue turning into life, the encounters
with the Princess?   These are all in the vein of pure
romance, touching life with strangeness and turning it
either into sheer beauty or grotesque fantasy.   There
is too in the early chapters, especially that ("An
Adventure on my own Account") in which Harry
describes his life with his father in London, a puzzled
small boy—

. . . in a house that, to my senses, had the smell of dark
corners, in a street where all the house-doors were painted
black, and shut with a bang.   Italian organ-men and milk-
men paraded the street regularly, and made it sound hollow
to their music.   Milk, and no cows anywhere; numbers of
people, and no acquaintances among them—

awaiting a mysterious and god-like father who acted
scenes in which "Great Will killed the deer, dragging

Falstaff all over the park after it by the light of Bardolph's nose"; there is in these passages a certain quality of the imagination that seems remote from our common conception of Meredith. It is the ability to reproduce childish recollections bathed in all the haze and glamour of a child's memory and imagination, which is the glory of the early part of *David Copperfield* and proof positive that its author, in spite of innumerable weaknesses, was a great artist. That quality of the imagination is there in those early chapters of *Harry Richmond*, and its presence, so unexpected, should remind us that it is dangerous to put limits to Meredith's genius.

The Egoist, as we have seen, is almost pure Comedy, with what we might call an undercurrent of romance. *Harry Richmond* is a romantic narrative, upon which Meredith tried, not very successfully, to graft Comedy. And all his novels could be examined with advantage from this point of view, as a combination of romantic narrative and Comedy in various proportions, but there is only space in which to notice one other, a story that is unusually successful in merging romance into Comedy. That is Meredith's own favourite, *Beauchamp's Career*. It begins in the old way, a glimpse of our hero's boyhood, and very quickly plunges us into scenes of great romantic interest and even beauty. The Venetian chapters, and the broken idyll they frame so exquisitely, would be almost intoxicating if it were not for a sobering touch of irony here and there. War, a frustrated youthful passion, then a political candidature on the Quixotic side; all this before the story has gone forward more than a quarter of its way; it would seem as if we were plunged into nothing more than the romantic life-history of Nevil Beauchamp. But very soon we perceive that we are in the middle of a Comedy, and yet we have not felt any transition, any clash of atmospheres. And we are in the middle of a very elaborate Comedy, perhaps the most elaborate of them all. The actions and interactions of the leading personages are amazingly complicated, so much so that at least four or five of the characters can be said to have Comedies of their own. Thus, to take only one instance (and it will also serve as an example of a characteristic Meredithian situation), there is the marriage of Rosamund Culling and Everard Romfrey. Beauchamp has quarrelled with his uncle, Romfrey, because the latter refuses to apologise to Shrapnel, the innocent victim of his thrashing. Rosamund, who has a maternal passion for Nevil, is distressed at this, and is willing to become Romfrey's wife, if she is asked, partly because she feels that she can bring uncle and nephew together again. Romfrey, on his side, determines to make her his wife so that he can beget an heir to the estate and thus neatly revenge himself on Nevil, a stroke that Rosamund, who accepts him, completely overlooks. They are married and soon an heir is actually on the way. But now Rosamund is so distressed at the breach between her husband and his nephew, and Romfrey himself is so anxious that nothing should disturb her, that he is compelled at last to make his apology to Shrapnel in order to make his peace with Nevil. He is lifted sky-high by his own petard. The very safety of the coming child, itself his revenge, compels him to do all the things he wished to escape from doing. And the child, when it comes, lives for one hour. Such ironic reversals are frequent in Meredith.

But this situation is only one out of scores in *Beauchamp's Career*, whose figures cross one another in intricate mazes of motive and action. If the action is followed sympathetically from Nevil Beauchamp's standpoint, as most readers probably do follow it, it remains a romantic life-story with a tragic ending. But if the reader steps back, as it were, detaching himself somewhat from the principal figure and simply observing the whole scene, it plainly reveals itself as an amazingly elaborate Comedy. Even the ending, when Beauchamp, drawing near to contentment after so much running to and fro for himself and all his circle, after so many shifting patterns of talk and action, throws away his life saving that of a little ragamuffin, even the end of the tale can be seen as the last stroke of a Comedy now turned impatient and bitter, a sudden savage gesture of the Comic Spirit. It mars the tale, just as the ending of *Richard Feverel* mars the tale, because it is out of key, like a splash of black or crimson oil paint in a water-colour. There goes along with it too that huddling away of the personages noted earlier in this chapter, an impatient sweep of the author's hand at the very last that can be found in almost every one of the novels. We feel that Meredith, having piloted his characters through their last big scene, is suddenly sick of the whole business and so makes an end of it, knocking one or two of his creatures on the head almost out of sheer perversity. But, in spite of its ending, *Beauchamp's Career* must be regarded as one of his most successful fictions, just because the two elements of romance and Comedy are so cunningly blended, the Comedy being prepared, by a touch here and there, even while

the romantic interest of the earlier chapters is at its
height.

We have seen that Meredith brought to fiction a
mind at once highly poetical and deeply philosophical
and critical, but lacking all those middle qualities that
seem to make the novelist. This not only explains the
form taken by his fiction, as we have already noted,
but it also explains certain curious characteristics in the
substance of it. He shows us a picture that has in it
no middle distance. Either we see his people as little
puppets illuminated by lightning flashes of wit, or we
are almost inside their minds, swayed hither and thither
by their lightest emotions. Compared with the world
of the ordinary novelist, his is a world revealed to us
either by sudden glimpses through a camera obscura or
by X-rays, but never by common sight. That is why his
novels seem so brittle, abstract, and unreal to so many
readers. They seem to have less connection with time
and place than any novels of the century. The mass
of stuff that takes up so much space in most fiction and
gives to most readers an illusion of reality, the multi-
tude of things, the houses and streets and furniture, the
incomes and bank balances and loans and mortgages,
the tangle of business and professional relations, is
entirely missing from Meredith's fiction. When we
put his canvas beside the crowded scenes of Dickens
and Thackeray it seems empty. Compare his world
with that of Trollope and the two seem more widely
different than Venus and Jupiter; they hardly appear
to overlap in any particular. Indeed, Meredith and
Trollope split up the whole range and scope of prose
fiction between them and represent the two poles of
the art. The scene of Meredith's novels seems no

nearer this ordinary world of "offices and the witness-box" than Shakespeare's Arden and Illyria. It is not that there is no background at all; there is always something waiting there for the significant moment—moonlit winding roads, high and glistening Alps, a wild-cherry tree in blossom, no novelist has shown such things so vividly and memorably. But there is no well-filled middle distance. Never was there a less "documented" fiction.

There are two novels, an early one, *Sandra Belloni,* and, more markedly, a later, *One of our Conquerors,* in which he seems to have made a deliberate attempt to fill in the background, to make some use of those ordinary relations that engage the attention of most novelists; but the result is distinctly unsatisfactory. He only achieves a grotesque effect, at times suggesting neither his own world nor this one, but a bad imitation of other novelists'. Thus there is in parts of *Sandra Belloni* just a suggestion of bad Dickens, while in *One of our Conquerors,* which never for one moment brings to mind the later Victorian world it is supposed to represent, there is a curious suggestion of early Thackeray. It is more than likely that Meredith's fiction failed to interest the public for a long time simply because that Victorian public was saturated in the novel of manners and regarded Meredith's work as a faulty attempt to produce the novel of manners. Meredith had himself partly to blame for this, because, after the two experiments of *The Shaving of Shagpat* and *Farina,* he did set out with all the appearance of writing a novel of manners, using the framework of the conventional fiction of his time. Never, of course, was a novelist less a novelist of manners, in the usual sense of that term.   The qualities that make the reporter, the historian, the story-teller pure and simple, that create the substance of most fiction, are the hardest to find in Meredith's.

Once we remember the poet and the creator of Comedy behind these novels, their curious character-istics, their empty middle distance, their lack of ordinary relations and *things,* their want of "document-ation", of definite suggestions of time and place, can be accounted for without difficulty.   The poet in him is not interested in such things, but only in the height-ened moments and unusual states of mind, the lyrical outbursts that need, as it were, a clear space for them-selves.   He would be stifled in the kind of world a Thackeray or Trollope shows us.   Nor is his colleague, the writer of Comedy, really any more at home in such a world.   It is too tangled and crowded for his purpose. All that he requires are a few clear-cut figures posed against a simple background, a few Chrysales and Philamintes, Maskwells and Mellefonts, in a trim world emptied of most of its interests and relationships, where Vanity may be hunted down in a clear intel-lectual light.   As soon as Meredith turned playwright, he made at once for this world of artificial Comedy, but writing his novels within the framework of the common form of his time, the long crowded novel of manners, he had to compromise.   But the result was that he created for himself a new kind of novel, and thereby enlarged the scope of fiction.

What he did was to make the art more mobile, more fluid.   He bent and twisted the form to suit his own purposes.   More than one critic has told us when and with what publication the modern novel really began,

and the dates and the works are extraordinarily various.
So far as English fiction is concerned, however, there
can be no doubt that the modern novel began with
the publication of *The Ordeal of Richard Feverel* in
1859. In that novel, and those following, Meredith
presented us, as we have seen, with a world radically
different from those of contemporary novelists, a world
bathed in a dry intellectual light occasionally coloured
by outbursts of romantic sympathy, of almost lyrical
ecstasy, a world of Romantic Comedy, in which the
common substance of fiction, life as revealed to an
ordinary observer and described by a realistic reporter,
is entirely missing. And in order to do this Meredith
had to adopt a new method of telling a story. We have
already declared that he was no narrator, that the art of
story-telling hardly interested him; nor is it necessary,
if we cling to the common conception of the narrator
and his art, now to reverse the judgement. Yet he may
be justly considered as a great innovator in the art of
narration, for he brought into existence a new method
that did nothing less than begin a fresh chapter in the
history of the novel. It is a method familiar to all
readers of contemporary fiction, and yet, in spite of
inevitable new developments, he himself still remains
its supreme master and his fiction remains the supreme
example of its successful use.

This method describes the action, at all heightened
moments, not from the usual detached point of view of
a disinterested spectator, but, as it were, from inside
the mind of one of the actors, not as it appears to a
merely observant onlooker, but as it appears in the
consciousness of a character taking part in it. He gives
us not the fact but the fact coloured by emotion and

distorted by thought. Both the poet in him, wishing to express states of mind, or, as Bacon said, "submitting the shows of things to the desires of the mind", and the critic and philosopher, intent upon psychology, grappling with motive, the conflict in the very soul, stand to gain from this change in the point of view. Indeed, it is the only way in which they could adequately express themselves in fiction. And it is really something more than the subjective method now employed by nearly all serious writers of fiction, who make use of the consciousness of their leading characters and give us an inward drama of thought as well as an outward one of speech and action. Meredith does this, but he does not stop here; it is not that he merely tells us what his personages think and feel, but he actually presents the scene to us, if the situation should demand it, completely coloured and shaped by the emotion and thought of the character involved, so that the situation comes to us as it came to the character, we live in the scene and also live in the character. In such passages as that beginning "He had landed on an island of the still-vexed Bermoothes. The world lay wrecked behind," and elsewhere in *Richard Feverel,* narrative has taken a new turn, something has been added to the compass of the instrument. And it is this method that, for any reader prepared to make the slight effort necessary to appreciate the significance of what it is describing, gives to Meredith's fiction its peculiar force and brilliance.

Other and later novelists, following, willy-nilly, on Meredith's tracks, have given us highly subjective narratives of this kind, but none has risen to such heights of romantic wonder and ecstasy. The poet in Meredith, when the reins are loosed, outdistances them.

Yet he, being a creator of Comedy as well, was also able to accomplish something not attempted by or beyond the reach of other subjective writers. He was able to keep before us an intellectual background against which all his figures move, which compels us, as we saw in the last chapter, to follow the searchlight of the Comic Spirit with a philosophic eye. Thus, to turn to *Richard Feverel* again as the nearest example of the method, even in those wonderful early passages that describe youthful passion as it has never been described elsewhere in prose fiction, we are conscious of that intellectual background and remark a certain bitter-sweet flavour of irony that does not destroy the romantic appeal and yet prevents us from losing our heads and with them our hold on the Comedy. In examining Meredith's idea of Comedy, in the last chapter, we saw how it contrived to bring together romantic figures and an intellectual background, a sympathetic interest coupled with a detached point of view, and thus achieving a curious dichotomy, self turning to examine self. It was his task (though not necessarily a conscious deliberate task) to work out this idea in prose fiction, and now, having examined the scope and form of that fiction, within the narrow limits of our space, we can see how he accomplished that task. We have now disengaged the aim and attempted to measure, with due regard to that aim, whose value has already been discussed, the achievement. It only remains to estimate, briefly, not from the standpoint of its author's aims, but from the standpoint of literature, of the whole tradition of the novel, the value of that achievement.

CHAPTER VII

THERE is much to be said for the practice, now out of
favour in criticism, of dealing systematically with a
novelist, totalling his faults on one side and his virtues
on the other, giving him good or bad marks, as it were,
for construction, creation of character, wit and humour,
descriptive power, and so forth. The weakness of this
formal method is that after all its labour it frequently
fails to give us the essential character of a writer, just
as the details on a passport or in a police *dossier* do not
really present an adequate portrait of a human being.
Its advantage is that it does succeed in clearing ground
woefully cumbered with vague and unsystematic praise
and detraction; it does tell us what goods our author
has brought to market. And as Meredith is a novelist
who has been almost buried under such vague and
unsystematic praise and detraction, whose goods, stored
away in an unusual bulk of complicated work, are
therefore all the more difficult to weigh, measure, and
value, there is a great deal to be said in favour of
reviving the method and applying it to him. We have
been at some pains to discover the essential character,
the form and scope of his work, and if we could
now formally tabulate its virtues and defects, thereby

removing so much thick undergrowth of criticism and letting in the daylight, the task of exposition and valuation would be admirably rounded off. Unfortunately it is not possible to do this. The peculiar character of Meredith's fiction prevents our formally tabulating its strength and weakness because its virtues and faults do not naturally group themselves as those of many authors do. He is pre-eminently a writer who has the virtues of his defects and the defects of his virtues. They follow closely on one another's heels. Thus, at the beginning of the last chapter we recognised —what was obvious to any reader—his weakness as a story-teller in the conventional sense, and yet before the chapter was done we were compelled to recognise too that he was a great innovator in the art of narration. And into whatever compartment we should follow him, those compartments beloved of formal criticism, such as characterisation, descriptive power, wit and humour, style, and so on, we should find this contradictory double character, this opposing strength and weakness.

He is an extremely faulty story-teller and yet contrives to enlarge the whole scope of the art. The bulk of his characters, that is practically all the secondary figures, are not created nor even constructed; they are mere names and dialogue and nothing more, without any hold upon our imagination; and yet he who has given us so many of these creatures of straw has also given us some of the greatest figures in fiction, some heroines inferior to none but Shakespeare's. His style is such that it cannot always cope with the expository and other matter that forms the ground level of fiction, the kind of matter that presents no difficulty to the ordinary novelist; and yet it shows itself capable of

handling the heightened moments, the great scenes, in
a fashion that lifts such passages far beyond the reach
of any but the great masters of the Novel. It is this
odd combination of weakness and strength that makes
Meredith a unique figure in the history of English
fiction. He is like a man who cannot pass the salt
without spilling it and yet is able to juggle with six
plates and the whole cruet. The very things that have
always been recognised as the most difficult things to
do in prose fiction, such as the creation of a real heroine,
the subtle exhibition of character dramatically, the
handling of highly poetic moments, he can do magnificently and with apparent ease. What he cannot do
successfully are the very things that we find done to
perfection in the ordinary intelligent novel, the very
commonplaces of fiction. This is in part due to the
fact that his pride forbade him to take any interest in
the commonplaces, in what any Tom, Dick, or Harry
could do fairly well. He was always too self-conscious
on this score to be a really great artist, for the really
great artist, forgetful of everything but the work in
hand, does not wonder whether he is being original or
merely commonplace and platitudinous, does not try
to be different from other people, but merely does the
work as well as it possibly can be done.

A great many of his defects proceed from this self-
consciousness. His later novels are almost ruined by
the writer's obvious desire to avoid the commonplace.
As he grew older he coddled himself and frankly
abandoned himself to his pet mannerisms. His pride
would not allow him to state a plain fact in a plain way.
In much of his work he was compelled to appear somewhat obscure simply because he was trying to express

really subtle and difficult impressions and states of mind. But by the time he came to write *One of our Conquerors, Lord Ormont and his Aminta,* and *The Amazing Marriage,* he had to give an appearance of subtlety and difficulty whether there happened to be anything subtle and difficult to express or not. His style had mastered him, and the reason why it was allowed to master him was that his genuine artistic impulse was by this time weak, whereas his pride, his self-consciousness, his desire not merely to be "different" but to be increasingly more "different", to be more and more the Meredith whom the public had neglected and his friends had adored, were stronger than ever. It is generally supposed that these later novels of his are more subtle and complicated than the earlier ones, but actually they are nothing of the kind. They are not more but less complicated than *Richard Feverel, Sandra Belloni, Beauchamp's Career,* and *The Egoist;* they are far simpler in conception, the action is less involved, the thought and feeling less subtle, and therefore they demanded simpler treatment. But this is just what Meredith would not or could not give them. Either he was by this time the slave of his own mannerisms, or he deliberately covered up this interior simplicity with a surface complexity, determined that it should not be said that George Meredith was at last coming to terms with his hostile critics and the public.

But while many of his defects proceed from this self-consciousness in the man himself, not a few of his weaknesses appear to be the result of a lack of self-consciousness, a want of it not in the man but in the artist. In considering the way in which the novel developed in his hands, we have said that he did this and did that, but it must not be assumed that he was always fully conscious of what he was doing. There is about him not a little of that casual air which is typical of so many of the greater novelists of his century. A touch of that almost reverent deliberation which we find in Flaubert and Henry James would have left his work vastly improved. Remembering what he did with the form, we cannot say that he did not take his fiction seriously, but we can say that if he had treated it with even a little more respect than he did, most of its minor faults would have disappeared. It may be, of course, that the root cause is to be found in the very shape and nature of his mind, for the same faults appear in his poetry, which lay next to his heart, and it would seem that Meredith, for all his amazing powers, had little or no instinctive sense of form. Thus, many of those minor faults in his fiction are the result of the writer's faulty sense of proportion.

Time after time in the novels he irritates the most admiring reader by throwing a disproportionate emphasis upon relatively unimportant characters, situations, and topics. He could detach himself sufficiently to lay down the general lines of construction, but having done that, he could not resist the temptation to make his novel reflect his interests of the moment even if it meant that the narrative would be knocked out of shape, its progress held up, its appeal considerably weakened. As time went on, he made less and less effort to resist this temptation, with the inevitable result that not only are his novels badly proportioned, but that, ironically enough, he himself, this hyper-sensitive chronicler of a hyper-sensitive social life, becomes at times that thing he most dreaded, a bore.

The difference between John Bull and his neighbours,
national defence, the Celt (whoever he is), the approach
of these and similar topics after a time makes the
reader's heart sink, for he knows full well that the
whole story will be held up, character, motive, and
action thrown to the winds, while Meredith treads the
familiar round of strained epigrammatic generalisation
and comment, turning himself into something perilously
resembling the creatures who make a desert of club
smoke-rooms.   That fine tragi-comedy of love and
public opinion, *One of our Conquerors,* is almost ruined
by the crowds of unimportant and uninteresting characters and the floods of unnecessary talk let loose upon
it. If Meredith would only leave us with Nataly and
Victor, Nesta, Dudley Sowerby and Dartrey Fenellan,
as he does in such a magnificent chapter as "Nataly in
Action", all would be well, for there is here some of
his most subtle and moving writing. But he crowds
us out with creatures we do not want to know, whose
opinions we do not want to hear, patriotic clerks,
epigrammatising authors, musical clergymen, vege-
tarian females, critical German visitors whose every
sentence weighs half a ton; and Nataly's trim ship
almost sinks under their weight. It is as if he were
trying to graft on to the original delicate tragi-comedy a
Peacock novel that has the usual mechanism of Peacock
but little or none of his clean-cut verbal dexterity and
humour.

The contrast between the heroine of this novel,
Nataly (for she and not her daughter, Nesta, is the
central figure), who combines the poetical enchantment
of some legendary queen with more than the reality of
the woman who lives next door to us, between her and

her nondescript crowd of guests, characters made of
paper and ink, is a typical example of Meredith's
strength and weakness. He does the supremely difficult thing well and the easy thing very badly. Any
competent serious novelist could have filled Nataly's
house with credible and not unentertaining characters,
whereas there are not more than four novelists who
ever lived who could have created a Nataly. And this
curious inequality runs through all Meredith's creation
of character. He could fill his novels with middle-
distance characters that are far less convincing and
interesting than those of the average serious novelist,
and here and there, too, he will give us a full-length
portrait, over which he has clearly taken pains, that is
a total failure. On the other hand, his finest characters
have been so intensely imagined, have so much vitality,
that they live in our imagination, like all really great
characters, as creatures larger than life-size, human
enough, as Falstaff and Macbeth and Cleopatra are
human, and yet, like them, having in them—as Meredith said of his great scenes—"a pitch considerably
above our common human". These are the characters
with whom he lived so long and intimately in his
imagination, as we saw in a previous chapter; the
Countess de Saldar he created out of his memories of
a vivacious aunt from abroad; the Richmond Roy he
used to interview in his study and over whose account
of the blood royal, as he once told a friend, he would
roar with laughter.

Once more there is everything here but mediocrity,
ordinary unassailable but uninspiring efficiency. It
would seem as if that world of his, that electrical
atmosphere, either condemns its creatures to be jerky

puppets, something lower than human beings as commonly reported, or dowers them with a superhuman vitality, a full and glorious life. It would be easy to exaggerate this contrast—and possibly we are doing so already—but a glance through his *dramatis personae* will show us what extremes he touches and how he avoids the common level of ordinary credible representation. The semi-allegorical experiments of *The Shaving of Shagpat* (that terrific *tour de force*) and *Farina* are hardly concerned with character and may be dismissed. When we turn to the novels proper we find that the characters tend to group themselves and can be best examined in groups. Thus there is a large masculine group of figures who meet with the approval of the Comic Spirit and escape its lash, who are more or less mouthpieces for Meredith himself, who rarely occupy the centre of the stage but are presented as standards of measurement in character. Austin Wentworth in *Richard Feverel*, Merthyr Powys in *Sandra Belloni*, Whitford in *The Egoist*, Redworth in *Diana of the Crossways*, Dartrey Fenellan in *One of our Conquerors*, Matey Weyburn in *Lord Ormont*, all belong to this group, and it is worth noticing that, as time goes on, Meredith transfers what might be called the hero's part, played in the earlier novels by dashing young romantics (who do not escape the Comic searchlight), such as Richard Feverel, Evan Harrington, and Harry Richmond, to one of these well-balanced and philosophical gentlemen. Their fault throughout is, as we saw in considering Meredith's idea of Comedy, that they are stiff and somewhat lifeless, taking no hold upon our imagination. They have been created, or rather put together, with the approval of Meredith's intellect rather than his imagination, and are indeed embodied points of view, only one degree more vitalised than the sapless creatures of a philosophical dialogue.

Then there is another group of characters, mostly to be found in the earlier novels, who have come in for more praise than the philosophical walking gentlemen, but who are actually even less entitled to it, being a source of irritation rather than pleasure. These are the eccentric-humorous personages, not to be confounded with the victims of the Comic. *Richard Feverel* shows us Mrs. Berry and her Benson (not to mention Hippias and other grotesque outlines); *Evan Harrington*, the Cogglesby brothers and Jack Raikes; *Sandra Belloni*, Pericles, Mrs. Chump, Braintop, and others; *Rhoda Fleming* gives us old Hackbut. All these characters are alike in the fact that they do not, from any point of view, justify the space they take up in their respective narratives. They are not credible (with the exception of Mrs. Berry, who can also be amusing, but there is far too much of her), nor are they very entertaining. They are failures. And they are failures of a curious kind, for they all suggest, though in various degrees, that their creator is working under an alien influence, that of Dickens. In later life Meredith dismissed Dickens, very uncritically, as an ephemeral popular novelist, but there can be no question whatever (even if we remember—what we are frequently apt to forget—that the fiction of the 'thirties and 'forties in general, which Meredith must have read when he was young, is touched with what we now consider the Dickens manner) that the influence of Dickens is there in his earlier work. Such a character as the elder Cogglesby in *Evan Harrington*, with his elaborate eccentricites, his gruff benevolence, his motive-less plotting and irritating air of mystery, might have stepped straight out of Dickens. And the trouble with these eccentric-humorous characters is not only that they are Dickens, but that they are also bad Dickens, reproducing what is most irritating, incredible, and mechanical in him. Meredith had to go another way to work before he could really create character.

He did, as we have already seen in the chapter on his Comedy, by putting not a little of himself into the characters. All his most memorable figures, his heroines apart, are alike in this, that though they may be there to be satirised, to be whipped with laughter, there is certainly not a little of George Meredith himself in them. He may have thrown off any allegiance to their ideas, but he could enter fully into their lives and minds; and while his intellect was preparing to chastise them, his imagination was enjoy-ing them. The two noteworthy exceptions would seem to be Squire Beltham in *Harry Richmond,* and Everard Romfrey in *Beauchamp's Career.* These two hard-bitten, plain-speaking, fox-hunting squires of the old school are magnificently alive. Every word they speak positively rings with truth. Yet there can have been little of Meredith himself (except his sharp dogmatic temper) in them, and they must be considered, at least on the masculine side, the best examples he has of close observation. But the others who stand out, the selfish wits, snobs, and egoists, owe their extraor-dinary vitality to his secret imaginative sympathy. It is the characters of this type who, at first standing on one side, become more and more the centre of the Comedy, until we reach Sir Willoughby Patterne. The first of them is, of course, not Sir Austin Feverel, who is only a stilted sketch, but his nephew Adrian, the "Wise Youth". *The Ordeal of Richard Feverel* would still be a fine love story even if there had never been a "Wise Youth", but without the intervention of that epicurean young gentleman the Comedy would lose nearly all its sparkle. His wise saws and instances, his bland retorts (such as that after Richard's statement that Lucy had done all in her power to prevent their marriage: "Not all! not all. She could have shaved her head for instance"), his malicious enjoyment of the whole Comedy as he sees it, and his occasional attempts at stage-management of it himself, such as his distribution of the wedding-cake to the relatives, are the very champagne bubbles of the Comedy.

The next to follow is that lady who is the mainspring of the action in *Evan Harrington*, the delightful Countess de Saldar. There are critics sentimental and naïve enough to dislike this character because she plays such a detestable part in the story, but the more often we read the novel, the more she gathers to herself our interest. Never was snobbery served with such wit, charm, energy, and courage. To see her at work, learning how, when she heard from her bedroom three young men talking of "the snipocracy", she "put on her bonnet hastily, tried the effect of a peculiar smile in the mirror, and lightly ran downstairs" to make a countermove, is to care little whether the love story, charming as it is, perishes at her touch. There is no one of an equal Comic stature in *Sandra Belloni*, *Vittoria*, and *Rhoda Fleming*, but after that we come to *Harry Richmond*, which is but a framework for that incomparable creature, the only fit mate for the

Countess, Richmond Roy. Though compelled to play the central part in what is really a satirical comedy imposed upon the romantic autobiography, Richmond Roy is, as we have seen, really a humorous character, a Micawber taken from low comedy and transplanted into high comedy, a world that, excluding its vitality and rich fantasy, is the very opposite of Dickens', an aristocratic world of wit, fine airs, and romance. This is not to say, of course, that Richmond Roy actually owes anything to Micawber, for, so far as any model was necessary, Meredith found one in his grandfather, the "Great Mel" of *Evan Harrington*. (Incidentally, the "Great Mel" must be considered a unique character, for he contrives to dominate the whole narrative and is certainly one of the most memorable figures in the book, yet he is killed off in the very first sentence.) Richmond Roy is the "Great Mel" raised to a higher power. He is the greatest of all magnificent pretenders who use this world as a mere back-cloth; a regal and tragic mountebank; an impostor who is himself better than the thing he pretends to be; his own best dupe; one dash of knavery to three parts of glorious folly and high romance. He is an artist, not without genius, who uses as his medium not paint nor words but life itself, and his attempt to create a masterpiece is fore-doomed to · failure. There is in him that touch of universality and that suggestion of something done once for all, a definite apotheosis, which mark the really great figure in literature. And he is not merely described, he is shown; his charm, humour, wit, his extraordinary mixture of craft and romantic simplicity, are all displayed at length in a character so intensely imagined, so brimmed with vitality, that he imposes himself at once upon the imagination and remains there, no matter how fantastic he and his world may appear to cold judgement. He is the creation of a master.

Sir Willoughby Patterne is frequently regarded as Meredith's greatest character, but actually he is over-shadowed by Richmond Roy. Sir Willoughby is the central figure in Meredith's most characteristic and perhaps his finest novel, and therefore it would seem to follow that he is his creator's greatest character. But actually it does not follow. He does not make the Comedy of *The Egoist,* in the sense that Falstaff creates the comic parts of *Henry IV.:* on the contrary, the Comedy makes him. Thus we cannot imagine his having an existence outside it, as we can Falstaff or Micawber, or, for that matter, Richmond Roy, outside their respective chronicles. The greatness of *The Egoist* lies in the Comedy itself, the successful working out of the Comic Idea. It is a study of both individual egoism and universal male egoism, and Sir Willoughby serves for both, but the real sting in the Comedy lies in its indirect exposure of universal egoism, which led Meredith's young friend to complain that it was aimed at himself. Sir Willoughby somehow turns into Everyman before we have done with him, even though he still remains Sir Willoughby. And that is Meredith's triumph. But we are sometimes tempted to wonder if the Comedy, in its universal application, would not have been stronger if Sir Willoughby had been brought a little nearer to Everyman, had had fewer extenuating circumstances in his birth, upbringing, and type of mind. Was it necessary to make him such an obvious prig and snob, obvious, that is, not merely in the searching light of the Comic Spirit but from any

ordinary standpoint? By doing this, Meredith, working with one eye upon the universal application of his
satire, was only putting difficulties in his own way.
Sir Willoughby, of course, remains a masterly creation,
but he cannot be disengaged from the Comedy that
contains him, and he is difficult to estimate strictly as a
character. Under close scrutiny he turns into a series
of devastating situations, through which there flutters
some part of our very selves.

But his greatest triumphs in the creation of character
are, by common consent, his heroines, who have been
"swimming" now for years in whole oceans of analysis
and appreciation. His are the most enchanting ladies
that fiction, of this or any other literature, can show us.
As rapturous praise of their charms already exists in
sufficiently great quantity, there is little need to add to
it, but something must be said about these heroines.
An account of the part they play in the Comedy has
already been given at some length in the chapter on the
Comic Spirit. We saw then that Meredith's heroines
have a double function, just as he himself appears, in
his fiction, in a double capacity. The poet in him
sees in them glowing images of health and beauty, the
fruits of right living, lovely and loving symbols of
Earth. The critic in him uses them as a kind of test.
This gives them a very strong position, quite different
from that they occupy in most fiction. We can now
change the standpoint, no longer examining his Comedy
but looking at him as one novelist in a long procession
of novelists, and ask what it is that makes his heroines
so infinitely superior to those of previous writers. The
secret lies, of course, in his manner of presentation.
Earlier novelists were convinced that if their readers

saw their heroines clearly, it would not be necessary to *know* them; if every detail of the lovely face were described, then the character of the lady could be left misty and vague. Meredith simply reverses the process. He presents his women as definite individualities, clearly marked characters, and takes the greatest care to show us the springs of their action, to examine their motives. At the same time, having described the character, he leaves the lovely face and figure, as they should be left, misty and vague. He gives them a kind of aura, makes them move in a golden mist, shows us shining figures in which every man sees his own Helen of Troy. The poet in him, contenting himself with hinting at this and that touch of beauty, but too wise to build up one of those elaborate portraits so familiar and so fatal in the Novel, bathes his women in glamour. If this poetic glamour is effective—and it is effective—then the psychologist can set to work with the knowledge that every stroke will only strengthen the appeal of the character.

It is this combination of definite individuality with poetic glamour that is the secret of Meredith's heroines. Shakespeare's, with whom they have often been compared, have precisely the same appeal. Cleopatra, Rosalind, Imogen, and the others are distinct characters whose beauty and witchery are, as it were, created by our imaginations, as we read, simply out of the atmosphere surrounding them. And all Meredith's psychological richness and acuteness would be of little avail if he too had not been able to create this atmosphere, to bathe his women in light and make them move to music. His task is to obliterate the old easy sentimentalities of the sexual relation, to approach it

intellectually and make of it something finer and more
honest, to compel us to think and not merely to feel
about it; but in order to do this with any success, it is
necessary for him to raise the power of the relation all
round, to compensate us for the loss of those easy
sentimentalities by emphasising the poetic enchantment
of sex, otherwise we lose sight, amid all this intellectual
analysis, of the driving force behind it all. So while
he gives us more intellect in the matter, he also gives
us more poetry, and nothing is lost but the whole is
raised to a higher power. Had he been less of a poet,
less able, in some curious fashion, to suggest sheer
lyrical ecstasy in the middle of his analysis of motive
and action, his heroines would have been little more
than factors in an intellectual problem. But they walk
in light and music and loveliness. Before we know
anything of his Diana, we are told how "She makes
everything in the room dust round a blazing jewel",
just as we are told that Juliet's beauty "hangs upon the
cheek of night, like a rich jewel in an Ethiop's ear".

To pick and choose among these beauties, if we may
judge from the mass of criticism of them, is but to exalt
a personal taste and to provoke quarrels. But they
are not all conceived on quite the same plan. The
two early heroines, Lucy Desborough and Rose Jocelyn,
are nearer the conventional young miss of fiction, and
in them poetic glamour is more evident than definite
individuality. They are exquisite girlhood and little
more. Emilia, as we saw in a previous chapter, plays
a much greater part in the action of the story, but rather
as a kind of test or standard. Against the background
of the artificial and sentimental Poles, she stands out
as the natural child of Earth, lovely, free, spontaneous,

touched with a genius as native to her as breathing, her music the very voice of Earth. In *Vittoria,* where she is not really the same person, there are suggestions of his more mature heroines in her here and there, but the symbolic figure of Italian national genius in her overshadows the individuality of the woman. Rhoda Fleming, in that curious novel which always suggests a Meredith masquerading as a Hardy, is a powerful study of heroic natural (almost earthy) womanhood marred by faulty handling. Dahlia, though slighter, is a far more poignant and convincing creature, though her type of mind and circumstances cramp her creator. She is moving but not glamorous. Neither of the two women in *Harry Richmond* is quite successful. Janet never quite comes to life, whether as a greedy and selfish little girl or as a self-sacrificing mature woman. It seems probable that Meredith was never certain what he intended to do with her. The Princess, who, it must be remembered, is only seen through Harry's eyes, is like a pale water-colour sketch of Meredith's greater heroines; she is Romance itself, this pale princess in the old German forest, rather than an individual woman. We do not catch the deep throb of her heart as we do with his more vital creations.

With the next novel, *Beauchamp's Career,* we take a leap upward, not to Cecilia Halkett or Rosamund Culling, though both these women are admirably sketched, but to a character who actually takes up less space than either of them but is yet more intensely alive. That, of course, is Renée, who is equally bewitching as a young girl in Venice, "a delicate cup of crystal brimming with the beauty of the place", or as a mature married woman, making one last desperate throw for love. Renée is a French woman that the French themselves have been pleased to accept, a creature of sweet imperiousness and delicate fire, as French as our next heroine, Clara Middleton, is English. Clara is one of the earlier heroines more exquisitely turned and dowered with a finer intelligence. Under her spell we hardly realise how passive a rebel she is, how shrinking and wavering, how little she conforms to some of her creator's pet doctrines; nor, we imagine, does Meredith himself realise it, being himself head over heels in love with her. At the very sight of her name a host of lovely little pictures flash through the mind. We remember her underneath the wild cherry-tree:

> She had a curiosity to know the title of the book he would read beneath those boughs, and, grasping Crossjay's hand fast, she craned her neck, as one timorous of a fall in peeping over chasms, for a glimpse of the page; but immediately, and still with a bent head, she turned her face to where the load of virginal blossom, whiter than summer-cloud on the sky, showered and drooped and clustered so thick as to claim colour and seem like Alpine snows in noon sunlight, a flush of white. From deep to deeper heavens of white her eyes perched and soared. Wonder lived in her. . . .

She comes and goes like a breath of spring, whether she is racing Crossjay across the park, eluding the suffocating embraces of Sir Willoughby, or sitting with wet feet in a railway waiting-room; a faltering adorable creature. Older, paler, one of Love's ghosts and yet a warm and pitiful woman, is Chloe, the tragic heroine of the short story of that name, a masterpiece only spoilt by its compression, the too rapid change of key towards the end. And of all the later heroines, easily the finest, and certainly the most underpraised of them all, is Nataly, in *One of our Conquerors*. She is a mature woman, the mother of a grown-up daughter, and is presented convincingly as such, and yet there blooms in her all the glamorous girlhood of the younger heroines. Her situation, as unmarried wife and mother, attached to a man who invites the stabs of public opinion, is the cruellest in which any Meredith woman finds herself, just as she herself is the noblest of them, and the breaking of her great heart shivers the whole savage comedy into dust.

Of Diana, the most famous of these heroines, we have said something already. The weakness of her story is, as we have seen, that Meredith is trying to do too many things at once in it. Either he should have made more use of Mrs. Norton and her history or less. As it is, he makes just sufficient use to hamper himself. Diana is not Mrs. Norton, she is Meredith's own creation. On the other hand, her story is largely borrowed from Mrs. Norton's, so that Meredith begins with a greater part of his course marked out for him. The action does not really proceed out of the character. The Diana he created would not actually have done the things we are told she did, or if she would, then his account of her is false. She has been compared to Charles II., who never said a foolish thing and never did a wise one. Meredith, who probably felt the strain of this inconsistency, lavished more of his glamorous art upon Diana than upon any other of his heroines, and there are moments when he and she carry everything before them and criticism is hushed. But practically every important event in the story, from her marriage to Warwick to her affair with Dacier (who should have been made more attractive, but Meredith, with the end in view, could not afford to do it), pulls us up short; and we ask ourselves why she is doing this and that and discover no answer. And though she may have never said a foolish thing, she certainly says a good many irritating things. She is Meredith's chief feminine wit and epigrammatist, and she is one of the most strained of all his witty characters. Such characters are practically without exception a source of irritation in Meredith, because, in order to display their wit against what is nothing less than a background of witty comment, he has to heighten it unnaturally, to thrust their epigrams into the most tortured forms. When almost every character in a novel has wit and the chronicler himself is for ever witty and epigrammatic, it is dangerous to try and present a character that will stand out against such a background as a wit. The strain is too much. That is why we find Diana throwing off so many things like: "You recognise a verisimilitude of the mirror when it is in advance of reality. Flatter the sketch, Miss Paynham, for a likeness to be seen." If popular young Irishwomen always talked like this at the dinner-table, the practice of dining out would soon cease.

Mention of wit brings us inevitably to some consideration of Meredith's manner and style, round which so many battles have raged. To say, as some critics have said, that he is too witty is a curious grumble. There is not so much wit in the world that we can afford to accuse a writer of giving us too much of it. If Meredith were frequently witty when wit was not demanded, there might be some justice in the charge. A writer who described the death of a child in a string of witty epigrams, however admirable in themselves, might be convicted under this head. But Meredith practically always changes his manner, heightening his prose until it becomes almost a poetical instrument, for the more emotional moments. It is not that he gives us too much wit, too many epigrams, but that, particularly in his later work, he will keep up an apparently witty and epigrammatic manner that prevents him from making a plain statement but does not compensate us by giving us any actual wit, any real epigrams. He is too frequently occupied in providing us with a Barmecide feast of wit and profound comment; we note the elaborate gestures, but nothing arrives for the mind to feed on. Once more we see how he contrives to do the difficult thing and fails to do the easy one. Nobody has excelled him in witty and really subtle comment or in bursts of really brilliant dialogue, just as no novelist has given us more gorgeous and memorable poetic moments. But his manner and style, especially in the later novels, refuse to undertake what might be called the donkey-work of narration. He will go miles out of his way, giving us pages of what can only be considered sheer bad writing, in order to avoid making a few plain statements of fact, necessary for the conduct of the narrative.

One of his guests has related how, on one occasion, he was asked by Meredith if he would like "to lave" his hands. It is this "laving" that is the ruin of his style when he is not at his best. No other writer of anything like his genius, so crowded with ideas and the master of such a massive vocabulary, has ever indulged in such pieces of cheap verbal affectation. Practically all his bad passages, from those in which a genuine thought is almost buried under an elaboration of imagery, to those that are simply fancies tortured out of all recognition, cruel Euphuism, are clearly the result of an impatience with ordinary methods of statement. That such ordinary methods would not always serve his turn, that he was compelled to be different by the very nature of what he frequently had to communicate, is true enough, but it does not clear him from the charge of sheer bad affectation. He frequently wished to be different when there was no necessity to be different. If he has not a happy image on hand (and imagery at once daring and felicitous is the mark of his style at its best), he will press into service any metaphors that occur to him and swell them out monstrously. If the matter looks like being commonplace, then the manner is rushed into fantastic fancy dress. As an instance of a thought almost buried under unnecessary metaphor, there is that chapter opening in *Diana of the Crossways*:

> The Gods of this world's contests, against whom our poor stripped individual is commonly in revolt, are, as we know, not miners, they are reapers; and if we appear no longer on the surface, they cease to bruise us: they will allow an arena character to be cleansed and made presentable while enthusiastic friends preserve discretion. It is of course less than magnanimity; they are not proposed to you for your worship; they are little Gods, temporary as that great wave, their parent human mass of the hour. . . .

And so forth, the thought cracking under the strain of the imagery. Other examples come quickly to mind. There is that passage in the Prelude to *The Egoist* beginning—

> Who, says the notable humorist, in allusion to this Book, who can studiously travel through sheets of leaves now capable of a stretch from Lizard to the last few poor

pulmonary snips and shreds of leagues dancing on their toes for cold, explorers tell us, and catching breath by good luck, like dogs at bones about a table, on the edge of the Pole? Inordinate unvaried length, sheer longinquity, staggers the heart, ages the very heart of us at a view. And how if we manage finally to print one of our pages on the crow-scalp of that solitary majestic outside? . . .

Or such things as this from *One of our Conquerors,* a charnel-house of slain English:

Think as you will; forbear to come hauling up examples of malarious men, in whom these pourings of the golden rays of life breed fogs; and be moved, since you are scarcely under an obligation to hunt the meaning, in tolerance of some dithyrambic inebriety of narration (quiverings of this reverent pen) when we find ourselves entering the circle of a most magnetic polarity. Take it for not worse than accompanying choric flourishes, in accord with Mr. Victor Radnor and Mr. Simeon Fenella at their sipping of the venerable wine. . . .

We are prepared to overlook those single sentences and phrases that have drawn down upon themselves the wrath of so many critics, phases like "feeling a rotifer astir in the curative compartment of a homoeopathic globule" and "a fantastical planguncula enlivened by the wanton tempers of a nursery chit", because they may be accepted as Meredith's "fun", a verbal spree. But passages like the above are rank bad writing. Nor do they strike one as being the exuberant freaks of a prose master, larking with his instrument. If we met them for the first time, we should set their author down as some pretentious novice trying to write "above himself". And in most of these passages that is what Meredith is trying to do, for there being no Meredithian marble on hand, he is giving us super-

Meredithian stucco instead, preferring to parody himself rather than to lapse into plain speech.

But when all such criticisms have been made, what
treasures of witty comment remain. Poetry, humour,
subtle psychology, all crammed into a phrase, and he
gives us hundreds and hundreds of such phrases,
illuminating a character, a situation, like flashes of
lightning. Open the novels anywhere and they meet
the eye:

"Laetitia Dale!" he said. He panted. "Your name
is sweet English music! And you are well?" The
anxious question permitted him to read deeply in her eyes.
He found the man he sought there, squeezed him passionately, and let her go. . . .

And—

The gulf of a caress hove in view like an enormous
billow hollowing under the curled ridge.
She stooped to a buttercup; the monster swept by . . .

And again:

"Does one see everything in a mirror, Nevil?" said
Cecilia: "even in the smoothest?"
He retorted softly: "I should be glad to see what you
see", and felled her with a blush. . . .

These things are everywhere. What most intelligent
novelists would regard as a somewhat exhausting
excursion into the witty epigrammatic is merely the
ordinary level of these novels of Meredith's, the
common stuff of the narrative. If his Comedy had no
significance whatever, if there blew through his work
no great wind of poetry and romance, to read the greater
part of it would still be an intellectual delight as we
leaped from crag to crag with our athletic and agile
narrator.

It is not difficult to say many hard things about his prose style, which bears a close relation to his poetical one, already examined.   But his aim and method in fiction demanded such a style and could not have been achieved without it.   Undoubtedly it is far more deliberate than most critics would seem to imagine. There is a famous passage in *Beauchamp's Career* that describes Carlyle's style—

> His favourite author was one writing of Heroes, in (so she esteemed it) a style resembling either early architecture or utter dilapidation, so loose and rough it seemed; a wind-in-the-orchard style, that tumbled down here and there an appreciable fruit with uncouth bluster; sentences without commencements running to abrupt endings and smoke, like waves against a sea-wall, learned dictionary words giving a hand to street-slang, and accents falling on them haphazard, like slant rays from driving clouds; all the pages in a breeze, the whole book producing a kind of electrical agitation in the mind and the joints. . . .

and much of this may be applied to Meredith's own style.   He too worked to produce that electrical agitation in the mind.   He wished to disintegrate the ordinary prose mass, having much that was new to express, and then recombine the elements in his own way, making it far more elastic.   His style might be compared to that of the artists who paint only in little spots of colour, thereby creating an unusual impression of vividness and vitality.   His aim is always to present only the essentials of a scene and situation, what is obvious being ruthlessly cut away; and his actual style closely follows his manner of observation, for it gives us a succession of rapid direct statements that are entirely disconnected and without the usual links and logical forms.   The reader is pelted with impressions and observations that he must synthesise himself. If he is lazy, unresponsive to that electrical agitation, he will make little or nothing of the matter before him; but if he is keeping pace with the author, he will be constantly and delightfully thrilled. He will live, to the fullest extent of his capacity, with the actors in the scene, and yet, as we have seen before, will be able to see them against the novelist's background.

This disintegrating process in the prose of fiction, keeping step with an ever-increasing subjectivity, has gone much farther in our time than ever Meredith took it or would have liked to have taken it. The poet and romancer never died in him, and he took care never to let his prose lose all semblance of a fabric, never let it crumble into fine dust. Thus he could always raise it for the moments that demanded a fuller sweep, a larger compass in the instrument. At such times the staccato drumming of his short and swift statements will ebb out and music and colour will come flowing into the prose. From the time when he could write, in *Richard Feverel,* such passages as that beginning, "Above green-flashing plunges of a weir, and shaken by the thunder below, lilies, golden and white, were swaying at anchor among the reeds. Meadow-sweet hung from the banks thick with weed and trailing bramble, and there also hung a daughter of earth"; to the time, nearly forty years later, when in *The Amazing Marriage* he could capture the colour and light and majesty of the mountains in prose ("Dawn in the mountain-land is a meeting of many friends" and the passages that follow), he never lost his cunning in the larger compass of the instrument, never failed to touch the moments of wonder with beauty in his expression of them.

Remembering the long pageant of his novels, the love-story of Richard Feverel that begins in an English dawn and comes to its crisis in that storm in Germany, Evan Harrington riding through the summer night, the enchanted woods whose nightingale is Emilia, the mountain scenes in *Vittoria,* to mention only the first few of them, remembering this long pageant, it is not difficult to believe that if his attitude towards life were proved entirely false and pernicious, his philosophy a snare, his psychology a bore, he could still hold up his head as a master of romance.

Throughout his fiction, as we have seen, he was apt to do the easy thing, the journeyman's work, badly, and for this, however great our enthusiasm for the man and his work, he must be blamed, judged to be the faulty artist. But the difficult thing, approached with dread by most novelists, he did not only well but, in many instances, incomparably, scaling heights that have yet to be overtopped. That is why he is such a simple target for adverse criticism. Any reader who is acquainted with a few competent pieces of fiction can remark the faults in Meredith, for they sprawl at length, inviting comment. But a reader who can go no farther dubs himself incompetent. To go farther is to encounter Meredith's undeniably great, perhaps unique, virtues, and these cannot be estimated and appreciated as we run. Appreciative criticism finds in him a very full subject. The more often we read this fiction as a whole, faulty though it may be, the more we are astonished at its richness and virility. Dropping all talk of comedy and romance and subjectivism and narrative and what not, we may say that these novels, whatever else they may be, are a literary feast, crammed with good things,

the largesse of a marvellously rich and generous
personality, in whose house of letters it snows meat and
drink. We rise from a reading of this fiction at once
more critical, more sensitive, and more in love with
life than ever, braced and blessed, because it is the
testament of a rich and glowing experience, of a
personality that never relaxed its strong grasp upon life
and lived intensely all its eighty crowded years.

There are many signs from references to him in
recent criticism and, even more important, from the
absence of reference to him, that suggest that Meredith
no longer holds the position he did as a novelist twenty
years ago, and certainly not that he held thirty years
ago. At the present time he would seem to be the
most neglected of all the great Victorian writers. But
it would be a mistake to see in this later attitude
towards him, as some critics, not without malice, have
hastened to see in it, the genuine verdict of Time. He
died too recently to be anything yet but the victim of
friendly or unfriendly fashion. As it happens, the
fashion has been unfriendly towards him. We have
already touched on one of the reasons why he has been
comparatively neglected of late. He lived to a great
age, crowded with honours, the subject of innumerable
eulogies (many of them extremely silly), an oracle, a
demigod of letters. After his death, when all the
papers had printed the obituary notices and appreciations that had been in type for some years, there was a
natural desire to change the subject, and there followed
that silence, only broken by murmurs of detraction,
which has followed the death of more than one very old
and very successful writer. When the old age of an
artist has been loaded with honours, it usually happens

that his ghost is vexed for some twenty years by adverse criticism.   There were reactions of this kind, by no means unhealthy, before Meredith, just as there will be many another after him.

There are, however, other reasons why the pendulum of literary fashion should have swung away from Meredith. Long before his death the kind of novel he wrote had lost favour in the eyes of the more fashionable critics and students of fiction, who lost their hearts to the closely-knit, impersonal narrative that we imported from France.   The alert young novelists, breaking their shins everywhere over his obvious weaknesses, felt that Meredith could teach them nothing, and so turned their attention elsewhere. Fiction became more preoccupied with the technique of narration and, at the same time, became less ambitious in its grasp and sweep.   Meredith began to look like a clever sprawler, a brilliant amateur.   But there is another and more important reason why he soon lost favour.   The tide of thought turned against him. His death roughly coincided with a notable change in what might be called fashionable philosophy, a change largely brought about by philosophers like William James and Bergson, and after them the deluge of new psychologists and psycho-analysts.   There was a marked tendency to glorify impulse and the instincts, and an equally marked tendency to condemn the over-intellectualisation of life.   This was followed in some literary quarters by a very emotional and pseudo-mystical outlook.   Tourgenieff went out of fashion and Dostoievsky came in.   Dickens came to be deified by persons, surprisingly enough without any apparent sense of humour, who twenty years before would have condemned him root and branch. Fashionable literary circles, scenting the severely "intellectual" in Meredith, dropped him. Those readers who could discover, let us say, a prophet in Mr. D. H. Lawrence were not likely to supply an audience for Meredith's Comedy. His "hue was not the wear".

It is more than likely that the pendulum will swing back during these next five years. A generation younger than that which reacted against Meredith-worship will suddenly "discover" the novelist. It is, indeed, high time it did. There are more than a few signs that the kind of novel he made his own is coming back into favour with the younger writers. And as we saw before, in considering Meredith's attitude, not only does he not "date" but he is still abreast of the age, and perhaps in front of it. Nearly all the soundest things in recent thought have been sketched somewhere in Meredith. This generation of ours, that prides itself on "facing the facts" and expresses, in its fiction, an ironic disillusion, will not find the great Victorian living in a pretty toy universe of his own that it can crumple with a shrug. Meredith, too, is a facer of facts. But the difference is that he does not take refuge in complete disillusion, which is after all nothing but lazy self-coddling and twisted sentimentalism, but goes forward and lays hold upon life, making his attitude as positive as he can. It is precisely that bracing quality of his that is most needed now, and sooner or later readers of the younger generation will discover for themselves his health and sanity and will never let him go. Even now fiction, in the hands of some of the most brilliant young writers, shows a tendency to give us philosophical comedy

instead of the heavy flirtations with sociology we have
had so long. It shows no signs yet of blending acute
psychological criticism and poetic romance as Meredith
blended them, but it is returning to the mode, and it is
not likely that the master of the mode will remain long
in his comparative obscurity.

The direct literary influence of Meredith is difficult
to assess, but, perhaps owing to the peculiar character
of his genius, it does not seem to have been very
extensive, certainly less than that of such later novelists
as Hardy, Henry James, and Conrad. But the indirect
influence of Meredith has been enormous. As we have
seen, he enlarged the scope of fiction, gave it new
matter and a new manner, and when the history of the
Modern English Novel comes to be written, he should
be given a prominent place in it, not only as an original
genius but also as a highly important innovator, a man
who added a whole new octave to the instrument of
prose fiction. The modern novel begins with him.
Even Mr. Arnold Bennett, whose type of mind and
methods in fiction make him a hostile critic of Meredith,
is compelled to admit that he was "not the last of the
Victorian novelists, but the first of the modern school".
The very fact that his work, retaining its freshness and
vitality, does not "date" has made us overlook his
services to the art. We forget that *The Ordeal of
Richard Feverel,* in which there is all of Meredith,
though not fully developed, was published as long ago
as 1859 and was a contemporary of *Lovel the Widower,
Adam Bede,* and *A Tale of Two Cities.* The literary
historian who spends some time examining the processes
of fiction, the development of the art of narrative (and
literary historians seem singularly disinclined to do

anything of the kind), will discover that 1859 is a date of some significance. So far small justice has been done to Meredith as an innovator. Nor must it be forgotten that the Novel itself and the intelligent novelists who came after him owe him a debt of gratitude, because he did much to raise the status of the form and the persons who made use of it. He may not have approached the Novel with the prayers and fasting of a Flaubert or a James, but he did treat it seriously and made it the receptacle of so much "brainstuff" that all manner of persons, previously accustomed to relaxing their minds over a novel, were also compelled to treat it seriously. No longer could they use merely one quarter of their brains in reading fiction, which became something more than an aid to digestion or a prelude to a nap. In order to be read at all, the Meredith novel asked for the full and undivided attention demanded by other forms of literature, and thereby smoothed the way for other serious fiction. Meredith paid heavily for his pioneering, and novelists and critics of to-day, however irritating they may find his occasional antics and touches of sheer perversity, will do well to bear in mind that even those antics were not without their influence in making possible the modern attitude towards fiction and the modern novel itself.

Whatever may happen to his name and fame, he cannot but remain a splendid flashing figure in our literature. Those who can see nothing but his faults— and he had many faults as a man and an artist—declare themselves blind to genius, and even prodigal genius. That he was not a genius of the highest order goes without saying. His work is obviously without that universality, that appeal on many different levels, which mark that of a Homer, a Cervantes, a Shakespeare, or, in their own fashion, a Dickens, a Molière. It is not merely that his work does not reach perfection, for the work of greater men is equally faulty, but that in spite of its richness, its breadth and depth, it lacks, just as he himself lacked, that four-square humanity which we expect from the supreme masters. He will never be everybody's man. A whole range of emotions never seems to have found its way into his work, which wants that charity, that brooding tenderness for man as man, which would endear it to whole populations as yet unborn. But, when all is said and done, he remains a giant, even though a giant somehow so twisted by pride and wilfulness that he appears of lesser stature. He touches greatness at an extraordinary number of points. No English writer of his century cast a wider net; he is a philosopher, poet, and novelist; he challenges Thackeray and James on the one side of his work just as he challenges Browning and Swinburne on the other; and whatever he touches he makes his own; his thought is his own, so is his poetry, and as for his fiction, it is original in every particular, in scope, form, matter, manner and style. His blend of philosophy and poetry, wit and rhapsody, comedy and romance, is unique, and there are moments when, overpowered by his breadth and force, we see in him the only writer of the last two centuries who can be placed by the side of Shakespeare. But then there comes home to us his plain lack of the Shakespearean broad humanity, the unfailing sense of form and rightness of touch, and his uneasy self-consciousness, afraid of simplicity even when simplicity is demanded, taking refuge in a hard brilliance. Yet the fact that this comparison with Shakespeare should even be entertained for a moment, and it has been actually boarded and lodged by some writers of note, gives us some measure of the man's stature. An undeniably great but puzzling figure; a genuine poet and philosopher, on the heroic plan, who can dwindle at times into a mere fop; a rich genius in whom there is some curious streak of the shoddy adventurer; a man of Shakespearean mould crossed with the strain of a Beau Brummell; and withal the author of an astonishingly full, brilliant, and varied canon in prose and verse, and of at least one novel, *The Egoist,* that takes its place among the six best pieces of fiction in the language; whose splendid figure gives colour and light to his century as it flashes down the years; who will brighten the wits and lift up the hearts of innumerable choice spirits when we, who have been taking our foot-rule round him, are all dead and forgotten.

INDEX